Photo: Samantha Strutt

John Aduma, British Chevening Scholar, poet and a veteran journalist with industry prizes – Reporter of the Year, 1992 and Investigative Reporter of the Year, 1992 – was formerly chairman editorial board of the *Daily Times of Nigeria Plc*, 2000–2003; executive secretary, Foundry Association of Nigeria (FAN), 1997–2000; between 1994 and 1997, he was at various times assistant features editor, assistant news editor, head, property and environment desk and city watch editor at *The Punch*; senior correspondent, *The Independent Weekly*, 1993, and staff reporter with *The Guardian*, 1990–1993.

Educated both in Nigeria and in the United Kingdom, Mr Aduma attended Christ the King's School, Okpoma, Yala, Ogoja in 1969 in the former South Eastern State of Nigeria, now Cross River State; St. Mel's Primary School, Woleche, Ebo, 1971; St. Gabriel's Primary School, Ebo Ipuole, 1972–

1974; Christian Vocational Commercial School, Okuku, Ogoja, 1975; Faith Institute of Stenography, Shogunle, Lagos, Nigeria, 1976; and for his secondary school, he attended and obtained the joint School Certificate and General Certificate of Education (GCE), Ordinary Level at Aladura Comprehensive High School, Anthony Village, Lagos, Nigeria from 1977–1982; University of Ibadan Extra-Mural Studies, Department of Adult Education, 1983–1984; worked at Exam Success Correspondence College, Lagos, between 1983 and 1985, and he holds an MA in international journalism with specialism in environment from City, University of London; City Business College, London, 2005–2006; MA in English, University of Lagos, Nigeria; a BA (Hons) English Studies from Obafemi Awolowo University, Ife, Ile-Ife, Nigeria; post-graduate diploma in journalism, Nigerian Institute of Journalism, Lagos; specialist diploma in teaching English: Literacy and ESOL, Level 5; Certificate in Education and Training (CET), Level 4 and an Award in Education and Training (AET), Level 3, CONEL, London.

He is the author of the inspirational bestseller *The Diamonds Are Here, Lord Rumens* (ed.), and the publisher of *Vigilance* – the world's leading security magazine (www.vigilance-securitymagazine.com) and *Scorpion News Corp* (www.scorpionnewscorp.com).

Besides, he is involved in City, University of London's professional mentoring scheme as a Post Graduate Professional Mentor (PGPM).

Mr Aduma is currently a doctoral researcher at the School of Languages, Cultures and Linguistics, Centre for Cultural, Literary and Postcolonial Studies (CCLPS), SOAS, University of London.

Dedication

This book is dedicated to all the young persons of the world who, on reading it, will resolve to turn over a new leaf and help create a world free of knife and gun crimes, including other types of crime – violence, killings, injustices – and usher into our human community, universal altruism, justice and harmonious peaceful coexistence amongst all the peoples of the world and generally, the peace of God that surpasses all understanding in a 'live and let live world'!

John Aduma

BE A BEACON OF HOPE IN THE WORLD

A Message to Young Britain

*For Sue Ives-Mdiba (Mrs)
From the Author
Your Student
With Best Wishes*

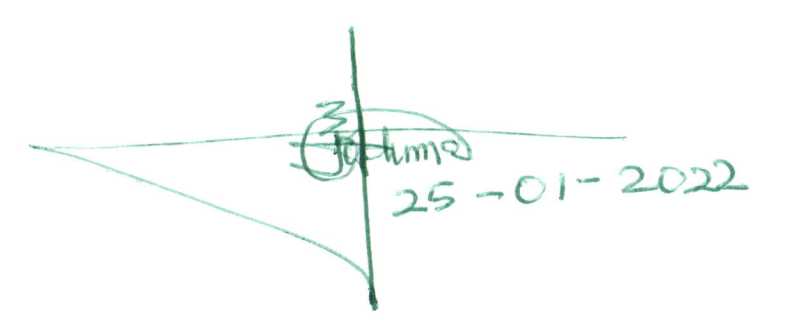

*Aduma
25-01-2022*

AUSTIN MACAULEY PUBLISHERS™
LONDON * CAMBRIDGE * NEW YORK * SHARJAH

Copyright © John Aduma 2022

The right of John Aduma to be identified as author of this work has been asserted by the author in accordance with section 77 and 78 of the Copyright, Designs and Patents Act 1988.

All rights reserved. No part of this publication may be reproduced, stored in a retrieval system, or transmitted in any form or by any means, electronic, mechanical, photocopying, recording, or otherwise, without the prior permission of the publishers.

Any person who commits any unauthorised act in relation to this publication may be liable to criminal prosecution and civil claims for damages.

A CIP catalogue record for this title is available from the British Library.

ISBN 9781528918381 (Paperback)
ISBN 9781528918398 (ePub e-book)

www.austinmacauley.com

First Published 2022
Austin Macauley Publishers Ltd®
1 Canada Square
Canary Wharf
London
E14 5AA

Acknowledgements

This book offers a rare opportunity for me to thank Papa, *Adamede* Aduma Ogri; Mama, Oji Eneyi Aduma (nee Wonah Ogbudu), for their excellent parenting and training me up in the way I should go in life and in my relationship with God; other family or sociocultural moderators in my upbringing, some of whom were my guardians whilst growing up included: Great Grandma *Ene* Odra Agrinya, Grandma Ogeyi Elo, Grandpa Ogri Ekawu, paternal Grandma *Ene* Ekawu Odey Omugbe, Odra Onwogidi, Wonah Onwogidi, Arija Onwogidi, Lega Onwogidi, and my elder sister, Ogeyi Aduma.

Other loved ones that I shall not fail to mention here are: Agbo Aduma, Ogri Aduma, Ogbene Aduma, Odey Ojeka, Aduma Ojeka, Oji Ojeka, Arija Okabo, Ofie Oleja, Okpagu O' Oko-Okpagu, Imaria Aduma, Ugbada Aduma, Wonah Aduma, Ochuole Ogri, Ogar Ohiero, and other members of my families, paternal and maternal, too numerous to mention here.

Also to be acknowledged are friends, former teachers and associates such as Neil and Margaret Pearce, Oloko Odey, John Ijoko, Ezekiel Shonowo, Jayne Okoroji, Linus Izor,

Peter Awotidebe, Rev Sola Aworinde, Mrs O.A. Alabi, Mr R.A. Adeoye, Anthony Omligbe, Chidi Umeh, Sumaila Ida, Oluremi Olaoye, Sunday Falade, Mukaila Popoola, David Okon, Paul Okoh, Rev Alan Beavis, Francis Akinwunmi, S.A. Adeyemi, Jimmy Ovuehor, John and Katie Smith, Sue Ives-Moiba, Pouri Mashoof, Bill Griffiths and Ms Samantha Strutt who took my headshot for this book.

Prologue

"Start children off on the way they should go, and even when they are old, they will not turn from it."

– Proverbs 22:6

Preface

Tears in my eyes, agony in my soul, pains
and anguish in my little corner, but...

*"Why are you downcast, O my soul?
Why so disturbed within me?"*

– *Psalm 42:5.*

When for the first time in Britain, I heard and read about young people stabbing themselves with knives and with other instruments of violence – and later to be pejoratively tagged by the British press as 'black-on-black violence' – my world was shattered and has so remained ever since at the spectre of young Britain cutting short their lives before their actual times here on Earth and worsened now that this bestiality and monstrosity has been allowed to become an epidemic of immense proportion, happening now at increasing and intractable regularity.

Therefore, the best way to begin the prefatory statement to this book on the epidemic of knife crime in the cities of Great Britain and, generally speaking, youth violence in the United Kingdom, is perhaps, to pose the questions:

- Why are they hacking themselves to death so young, leaving their loved ones and society to sorrow perpetually?
- And what happened to all their dreams when they died so young?
- How many more will die before we all join hands to stop this blood thirstiness amongst young Britain, eventuating in the free flow of the blood of young persons, which flows ceaselessly like the cascading waters of the Niagara Falls?

Personally, these are a few of the myriads of questions that usually do course through and predominates my mind each time a young person is gruesomely hacked to death very untimely. And continued to haunt my mind, have these bestiality, monstrosity and other behavioural tendencies of children and youngsters in public and private spaces since my arrival in Britain in 2003. My culture shock, you would say; for in Nigeria, children and young persons are brought up to respect the sanctity of life and the elderly.

My first noticeable difference between children and young persons in the United Kingdom and their counterparts in Nigeria/Africa was their general lack of environmental sensitivity as often displayed on buses, trains and in public places.

This total lack of sensitivity amongst young people in Britain, and their lack of respect for the other persons sharing any public spaces at any given point in time with them, are a daily occurrence in every public space they share with others, especially those slightly above them in age.

And a memorable one I have continued to remember till date, was an occurrence on a bus I was on, with some school kids, having their uniforms on, whilst I was returning from where I would later come to know as Elephant and Castle, to my then 15 Bastwick Street Residences of City, University of London, EC1V 3PE.

I generally do not like noise in my life, for its presence wherever I'm, gets me thoroughly disorganised and uncoordinated, resulting in a lack of concentration by me – and sometimes making me to become very irritant. But that was just what those school kids on the same bus with me and other passengers were doing. A hell of it for that matter, hitting and banging the bus, chasing themselves about on the bus!

The shock was that no passenger cautioned them as would have been the case in Nigeria as they continued with their unparalleled and uncouth mannerism, excitedly relishing in that strangeness without an iota of regard for the other passengers.

In fact, I must say they did, for have they not turned the bus to their world and Republic, and at the same time converting its inside into birds' sanctuary?

And screaming out, "Stop making noise on the bus," I had tried to quieten them, but rather than keeping quiet, they now increased the tempo of banging on the bus, hitting their legs thereon and began to scream the more, louder than ever and running up and down the bus.

Repeating my plea two more times, but to no avail, and with no support from the other passengers, I was left with no other choice than to alight from the bus at the next bus stop.

Out of embarrassment, I sneaked into the crowd to avoid being seen by the disruptive school kids and the other passengers, with the kids putting their heads through the windows yelling at me, as I wondered what the other passengers might be thinking of me.

But I wondered not only at the bad behaviour of the uniformed school kids, but also, at the seeming helplessness and subdued muteness of the other passengers. The kids were actually the ones in charge of the bus as till date, it is they who are in charge of every home in Britain as well as every public space in Britain.

"This is how kids in Britain behave," came a reply from everyone I had told about my baptism of fire. "They are not brought up to respect anyone, not even themselves."

This type of upbringing completely disregards the fifth of the Ten Commandments, which says, "Honour your father and your mother, 'that your days may be long upon the land' which the Lord, your God is giving you."

Again, youngsters are further enjoined thus by the holy scripture: "Children, obey your parents in all things, for this is well pleasing unto the Lord." – Colossians 3:20

Honouring and obeying their fathers and mothers is to be extended also to all those who are older than them in age, including having respect for institutions, constituted authorities and the laws of the land.

But do children in Britain honour their fathers and their mothers and respect institutions, constituted authorities and the laws of the land?

Answer: No!

Do they honour themselves?

Answer: No!

Do they honour constituted authorities and obey the laws of society?

Answer: No!

A few months later, I was to receive another shocker which has turned out to be a lesson for me ever since. A friend of mine – a fellow Nigerian – who also was with me at City University of London, at the time she and I were on our way to the Campus from my residence, when I told her, I was going to tell off a group of kids who were playing football right in the middle of Goswell Road, despite vehicles coming from both sides of the road. Then Miss Stella-Maris Ekpene exclaimed: "E–w–o–o–!"

"Don't you dare, Your Excellency!" She had warned me.

"Why not?" I asked.

"Those kids you never know what's in their pockets," she said. "Kids in this country go out with knives in their pockets."

"Why did they have to go out with knives in their pockets?" I asked to know.

But Stella was more after my safety and to discourage me from such meddlesomeness, although it was the right thing to do, to caution young people whenever they are misbehaving, and to challenge all their irresponsible tendencies and indulgencies, so came no answer from her as to the reason why kids in Great Britain do carry knives in their pockets. Anyway, how was she to know in the first place when both of us were new in the country?

My third kind of culture shock when I first came to the United Kingdom was the daily sight of seeing babies carrying babies about to Dalston Market on Kingsland High Street, directly opposite my rented apartment by the High Street above a Beauty Shop (43–45A Kingsland High Street, Dalston, London, E8 2JS).

That room above a beauty shop was, in fact, my first rented room after I had finished my Programme in International Journalism at City, University of London in 2004.

And the shocker lay in the fact that each time I put my head through my window, I would see a caravan of babies pulling about babies to which I had begun querying what I had then ignorantly regarded as the handiwork of irresponsible and indolent mothers, entrusting their babies to their children or allowing their underaged children to be carrying their siblings to the ever-crowded Dalston market, notorious for both human and vehicular traffic!

That concern of mine for the health and safety of the babies on buggies being carried about by their 'senior sisters' as I had then thought, went on for a very long time without me telling it to any of my friends, but the pain and turmoil in my soul disturbed and tortured me for a very long time.

Even though that pain has continued till the very present, and I must confess, has now become spiritually polluting to me – I mean the daily troubling sight of seeing mostly young persons of my community, who should be in schools, preparing for the beautiful future which to my mind lies ahead of them, are now to be seen carrying equally their own babies and 'not' their mothers', as I was to later learn through a Ghanaian friend of mine, then putting up with me, pushing them around on buggies and thus, bringing upon themselves responsibilities beyond their biological ages.

But how did I discover that these babies were not the babies of the mothers of the unparented baby mamas who were carrying them around and all over the place on buggies?

One day, when Mr Francis Amedzorneku, my room mate and friend, and I were in the house together because he was off from work that very day, I had asked him thus, "Who are these very irresponsible mothers that would allow their babies carrying these babies around like this all over the place?" But Francis, instead of offering me an answer to an epidemic that has been ravaging my mind then, and I would say again, till the very present, decided to make a 'fool' of me!

He started laughing and laughing, cackling and cackling with a sort of laughter that induced cough and tears from him at the same time, rolling on our then little bed – falling and falling on it, laughing and laughing, coughing and coughing, laughing and laughing and cackling and cackling, as if saying, "What an idiot, you must be, John," for reasoning so stupidly.

Out of wonder and unparalleled embarrassment, I asked him, "What's wrong with my question?"

And in profusion, I did query him, "Have I asked a silly question?"

But my Niagara Falls-like questions seemed to trigger more laughter from him.

It was only when he had finally got himself together, that he told me that, "The babies indeed belonged to the 'babies'!"

But I did not believe him, so I invited him to the window where I was standing, disbelieving what he had just told me about the baby mums.

"Look at them," I said, pointing my forefinger to the caravan of baby mums that were pulling about their babies on buggies as if on parade, or on a baby exhibition. And he started laughing again and reaffirming the babies on buggies, in fact, belonged to the 'babies' who were driving the babies around on buggies.

I drew in some air and heaved a big sigh of relief, but Francis noticing I was not convinced said I should ask a mutual friend of ours Reverend Fitzgerald Johnson, a Sierra Leonian, whom we were both expecting that day. And a few hours after he had arrived, it was Francis who broached the matter of the baby mums to him, telling Reverend Johnson I did not believe him when he told me that the babies on buggies, in fact, belonged to the 'babies' carrying them about.

"Yes," said Rev Johnson. "But how come you did not know before now?"

Reverend Johnson then started giving me a lecture on the baby mums, saying, "You can't find an unattached spinster to marry here. These baby mums are all over the place. In fact, about 95% of the girls you see around in this country are baby mums. If you want to marry an unattached woman, it will be very difficult for you to find one as all of them already have children."

Johnson shocked me further by not only corroborating Amedzorneku's truism but worsened my already saddened state by adding that a lot of them had two, three to five kids for five different men, if not more!

And not only this unseemliness, but he further added, "Even government gives them council flats after they have given birth to their babies as the government did not want these babies to be brought up in thoroughly congested rooms/houses with their parents. It all started during Margaret Thatcher's era. Once you have a baby, they give you council flat in which to live."

Having become a trend, youngsters – the baby mums who already have babies, as if having babies is a matter of going to a local supermarket and select a product – do often put their peers under undue pressures, urging them to go and get their own babies too, "Go and get your baby, what are you waiting for?"

In this condemnable shame, their boy counterparts would boast thus, "I gave Samantha a baby!" And another would boast, "I gave Kimberly a baby!" Others, "I gave Veronica a baby!", "I too gave Shanna a baby!"

Some are able to withstand these undue pressures but others are not able to, so like cocoyam leaves succumb to them. And the next time you see them – a protruding tommy!

However, very few who are able to proceed to the universities are put in a family way immediately after they have finished their studies by boys without any discernible means of livelihood.

Also, those who are able to withstand the pressures, albeit temporarily, but could not or are not able to proceed to universities are soon pressured into having babies, even whilst they are still babies by randy boys, hanging out on street corners, in alleys and subways!

Also, some parents, especially relatively young women in a hurry to have grandchildren who they will use to boast about in their community, do pressure their daughters into family life before they reach their biological time and are ready both psychologically and financially.

In 2006, whilst working in North London, I did hear a mother say to her daughter who was complaining about the congestions in their house: "Don't you know what girls of your age are doing to get council flats?"

Whilst discussing this societal complicity in the baby mums epidemic with a female member of my church, she corroborated my eyewitness account thus, "When I was eighteen, I wanted to get a council flat and I was asked, 'But you are not pregnant?'"

Another woman was heard saying to her daughter, "If you don't like him, just have sex with him. That's not the worst sin anyone will commit."

Added to this shame also, in the new British family arrangement is the prevalence of a practice commonly known and referred to as 'accompany'.

This is an arrangement whereby a man or a woman arranges or actually lures a woman or a man to 'give' them a child without being married to themselves and without living together – a sort of dog-type arrangement, where a male dog copulates with a female dog by the roadside, and having satisfied himself runs away, never to be seen by the female dog anymore!

In fact, a female friend of mine who once gave me an invitation to visit her in her house, although I couldn't get to honour the invite, had said to me, "…John, you know I have to make a baby every year."

But why would she want to make a baby every year?

In her own case, she has already been rewarded by the state, although, at the expense of the taxpayer, having had two children outside of wedlock. Besides, there are a 'well done' allowances/benefits to get from the state on each child she had brought into the world without prior planning and preparation!

These state rewards for baby mums and baby dads are, in fact, what have been encouraging kids into this condemnable unwholeness at the expense of the toiling masses of Great Britain.

A baby brings a baby into the world when she is supposed to be in a class, learning and preparing for the very bright future that awaits her, if only she can be patient, and is rewarded with a council flat.

So, why does anyone out there think this condemnable act, although, not condemned in Britain but condoned, shouldn't become an epidemic as it is currently?

Why does anyone think this very behaviour which once did lead to excommunication of the persons involved by both the Church and the entire society in Victorian England, shouldn't now become a sort of 'Ebola' disease amongst young persons, taking their attention away from their education and their future – all for the rewards of a council flat and the 'well done' benefits attached to this shame?

And i must say, I'm in tears for my own community, where unarguably, there is a preponderance of this shame and as a person of African descent, I want to remind all my brothers and sisters – the Afro-Caribbeans – that this very ugliness has its roots from slavery and must not, repeat; must not be perpetuated in the 21st century and taken beyond.

All concerned must be made aware that this could be a ploy and at the same time a bait by the state to make this very community non-competitive, eventuating in the epidemic of evidently very high rate of dysfunctional families amongst them as unarguably is the case now.

In certain quarters in Britain, babies have become just toys and this must not be allowed to continue any more.

Therefore, all young persons in Britain need education as to when and how to bring children into the world. In most cases, these kids are brought into the world with just a box of chicken and chips, and a bottle/can or a cup of soft drink, followed by a three minutes' pleasure in the alley or in the subway.

Babies of school-going age bringing children into the world is bad enough. Worse, baby mothers and baby fathers need parenting, but there is none.

However, what there actually is, is what I call zero parenting! So, who then parents the baby mother's baby?

It is thus, the candid opinion of the author that after an aggressive drive to educate young people on the need to start a family only when they are ready physiologically, biologically, psychologically, sociologically, culturally and financially, and failing by any to heed the advice of government, society, community, the school, the church and the mosque, such young people must be left to bear the consequences of their ungovernable concupiscence and lasciviousness.

Therefore, the policy of rewarding this shame with a council flat and going on to allow them access the various allowances attached thereto, must not only be reviewed but be stopped forthwith.

Young Britons must take the word of the preacher on board that there is time for everything. And they must henceforth not use or be seen to be using the time when they are supposed to be in class learning, thinking of a career and planning their future to be nursing babies and carrying them all over the place on buggies. A word is enough for the wise!

And let me send my eternal message to all the young persons of Britain and those in other nations of the world that 'enough is enough' of this folly and ugliness.

It is not right for kids to be having kids, for kids who do not have any jobs whatsoever or any means of livelihood, and in most cases, still very much dependent on their parent/s, who themselves are living from hand to mouth, having homes in the most deprived densely populated areas of Britain.

In a situation like this, who fends for the kids they have brought into the world, not ready, not prepared and not mature? The taxpayer, of course!

If for momentary benefits, they compromise their future, it means they have eaten that future today, so should live with the scars for the rest of their lives.

The fifth Commandment clearly confirms the fact that God did not intend that a child be brought up by just a parent – whether man/father or woman/mother, but by both parents (husband and wife), and by extension, by the other family members and the society at large, all acting as mentors and moderators to the child.

However, the root causes of knife crime in Britain are multifaceted such that no right-thinking person will blame it on just a factor, how much more on single motherism as to do so will be very, very unfair to all single mothers/parents.

But from my own point of view, there are just four factors that have fuelled the epidemic of knife crime in the United Kingdom, viz:

1. Spiritual
2. Spiritual
3. Spiritual
4. And others.

And to come under my 'others' heading will be trillions of subfactors which are subjects of my next book. But in the interim, what should we all do collectively as a nation and as a people?

Answer: Get out what is inside the pockets of children and young people – those objects of sorrow, even the blades of shame and condemnation or make all of them to surrender that which is in their pockets very willingly, enthusiastically, lovingly and peacefully – so that the peace that surpasses all understanding will course through and flood our streets, cities, the nation and the world once more.

Therefore, it is hoped that whenever the trumpet shall sound, as it will soon go forth, summoning all young Britain and the world to the launch of the 'Global Youth Movement Against Youth Violence', you will be there.

God bless the United Kingdom of Great Britain;

God bless our world;

And may He also, bless the children of the coming generations of mankind!

Children and Youngsters as the Seeds and the Future of Nations and the World – How I See Them from My Little Corner

"Don't copy the behaviour and customs of this world, but let God transform you into a new person by changing the way you think. Then you will learn to know God's will for you, which is good and pleasing and perfect."

– Romans 12:2

I have always been interested in children and young people, whether in Nigeria or in Britain. In saying this, I'm aware it requires courage and boldness to publicly declare thus, in Britain, because of the nation's bad experiences with bad people in our midst who have chosen to exploit the innocence of kids and youngsters, whom they are supposed to cherish, love and protect.

This interest is first and foremost inborn – deposited in me by God before I was ever formed in the womb – Jeremiah 1:5 – and I don't think I will be able to tell the world and posterity the origin of this innatism and when and why my Maker and my Redeemer has chosen to deposit in me this divine seed, for the seeds of the world and the 'future' of the future of all of mankind.

Because this seed of God has always been there on the inside of me, even when it was not obvious to me, and from the beginning, and earliest ages, God revealed it to all around me to see, feel, recognise and appreciate, hence I was given the name: *Ada ayi ape* (Yala, for 'father of children') by my paternal grandfather, Ogri Ekawu, a legendary mystic; maternal great grandmother, *Ene* Odra Agrinya; maternal grandmother, *Ene* Ogeyi Elo; and later by an aunt of mine, Agbo Ogar, when I left Okpoma to live in Ebo with my elder brother, Anthony Wonah Onwogidi who was a teacher – God bless him for bringing me up in the way I should go, even though I hated such a very strict upbringing as a boy.

In fact, I reported him to Mama, Oji Aduma (*nee Wonah-Ogbudu*), and Papa, *Adamede* Aduma Ogri, and other relatives, who of course, did not reason my way.

I had groused against him thus, to our family members, "He always suffers me and doesn't allow me to play."

But looking back now as an adult, what I considered then as 'suffering' was the fact that he was wont to be giving me responsibilities, which are not given to many youngsters these days, especially at home, including whenever he was leaving Woleche-Ebo, where we were living, for Ebo-Ipuole, in addition, to ensuring I finished doing my school homework and the ones he himself had given me, with having a little time to play.

But I would, rather, then wish he did give me enough or more time to play, having the same degree and latitude /measure of time/liberty, enjoying such unfettered or borderless liberty to play around, wandering about, even though sometimes aimlessly as boys and girls of my age and generation had, and were enjoying their seeming borderless freedom, whilst he hemmed me in on all sides in between with his boundary setting for me.

Also, at Aladura College, Anthony Village, Lagos, Nigeria, that special gifting in me was so obvious to the entire 62 teachers and all the members of the nonteaching staff, just as it was to other people, wherever I had lived in Lagos, such that both at home – the various barracks I had lived in Lagos, the then airport headquarters at Ikeja in Lagos, which later became the air force barracks, Military Cantonment, Ikeja, Lagos, Nigeria, 41 Division Artillery Regiment, Ajara Topa, Badagry in Lagos and at Aladura Comprehensive High School, Anthony Village, Lagos, Nigeria, I was regarded by both soldiers and the barracks boys and other barracks residents and by my college teachers as a role model – a prodigious boy for that matter at my age, in addition to being a very gifted and brilliant boy – hence used as an example to other youngsters in these places, wherever I went and wherever I had lived.

In other places, I had lived in Lagos, after leaving Aladura Comprehensive High School, I was in more measure attracted to children and young people and this was to later earn me the fond name Uncle John amongst kids and youngsters in these places and in the neighbourhood, whereas the adults on their part fondly called me *Baba Ewe* (Yoruba, for 'father of youth') – and graduating therefrom, right from Aladura College as a mentor and counsellor for kids and young people – especially those whose upbringing by their parents had shipwrecked, those who have fallen out of line and out of favour with their parents and guardians, despite their parents' great efforts in positively parenting them, were all brought to me to counsel/mentor and at Aladura College, our teachers would encourage other students to emulate me and keep company with me.

And I thank God that virtually all such kids and youngsters whose paths and mine had crossed when they were off their rocker or out of line, were by God restored through me, but those who refused to heed the messages that God gave to me to give to them had very, very sad stories to tell, and some very sad endings.

It was, therefore, not surprising that after I became born again on 24 June 1984, I chose no other Ministry in which to join, but the Child Evangelism Ministry at the New Estate Baptist Church, 57 Adisa Bashua Street, Surulere, Lagos, Nigeria to serve along other brethren.

It was also at New Estate that a sister, Mrs Foluke Oke, who had watched that interest of mine in children and general enthusiasm in working in the Department that one Sunday said she would like to have a discussion with me after the Sunday service. And during the meet after the service, she suggested to me to consider studying Child Psychology whenever I wanted to go to the university to study.

She said, "I have watched you over time and I noticed you have a genuine and an unparalleled interest in children, and I think it will be good if you go and study 'child psychology' at the university."

Although, great as this idea was, when I went to the University of Ife, Ile-Ife, later renamed Obafemi Awolowo University, I did not study child psychology as advised by

Mrs Oke, but English Studies as a young and budding writer and offered General Psychology as an elective.

Also, at Ife, I was an active member of the Child Evangelism Ministry of the Evangelical Christian Union (ECU), a foremost Christian Students Fellowship. This was continued during my one-year national service in the Bendel state of Nigeria as a member of the Christian Copper Fellowship, Benin City.

As a corps member, that interest in young people led me to start a weekly column under a title given by the Sunday Observer editor at the time, Mr Jimmy Ovuehor, *For Posterity* as against *Guidepost* which was what I had intended to call the weekly column.

Introducing the column to all staff members of the National Youth Service Corps, state secretariat and the corps members serving in the former Bendel state during the period under reference – 1989–1990 – Mr S.A. Adeyemi in a circular letter – he had issued – dated 21 May 1990 and entitled: *Community Development Service 1990: A Column is Born*, wrote,

"I wish to invite your attention to page 13 of the Sunday Observer with the caption 'For Posterity' by Mr John Odey Aduma, a corps member. It is a weekly release by the corps member for the youths of this great nation. This column was born as a result of our call for CDS 1990 amongst corps members in this state.

Mr Aduma, however, works with The Observer but invariably turned a columnist in the name of 'All Year-Round Community Development Service'.

He is a soft-looking, humble, and industrious young man. He is a versatile and prolific writer who deals with inspirational thoughts that could better reorientate our youths. John bubbles with ideas and of course, he is a fast and fantastic writer who touches on various topics such as Philosophy, Business Education, Economics, Sociology, Political Science, etc.

This pen pusher has of late emerged an ardent counsellor of youths, as many of his readers have started pouring in letters for counselling and guidance from this young, sagacious and vast writer. I wish to assure you that by reading his column regularly, you will gain much knowledge and wisdom because the corper columnist is a scholar indeed."

- S. A. Adeyemi, Senior Inspector, Community Development Service.

The reader is to be made aware here that all the articles featured in the author's *For Posterity* column made up his first published book 'The Diamonds are Here'. And of that book, Air Commodore Emeka Omeruah, the Federal Minister of Youth and Sports at that time wrote, "The Ministry is very proud of young talents like you. Your initiative and bold pioneering attempt are quite commendable. It is hoped that our youth will draw a lot of inspiration from this book."

And barely three years after graduation from Ife, I was appointed to serve on the National Youth Committee of the Federal Ministry of Youth and Sports under Air Commodore Emeka Omeruah, with Mrs Ololade Oki (a.k.a. Mama Youth) as the National Director of Youth Development.

In fact, I was a member of the National Planning Committee that organised the 1993 National Youth Festival held in Ibadan, Oyo State, Nigeria, which saw Nigerian youths from the 36 states of the Federation, including Abuja gathered at the Liberty Stadium in Ibadan and inspecting the youth parade that year was the Head of the Interim National government, Chief Ernest Adegunle Oladeinde Shonekan.

It should be recalled here that whenever wayward children and youngsters were brought to me for counselling by their parents/guardians, I would frankly let them know that they knew me as Uncle John, but whenever I wanted to start talking to them, I would let them know that I would speak to them not as Uncle John that they usually know, but as 'a Prophet of God', in addition to taking permission from them as to whether to proceed in the talk or not, because once I started, it was not I that would speak, but the Spirit of God who would now speak through me to them, and if they chose to refuse what the Lord would pass through me to them, the consequences of that disobedience were usually very grave, but if they were wise enough to heed the word of God through me to them, it would forever be well with them, and concluding, they would never be the same again.

But here in Britain, even though that holy and divine bond between kids/young people and me remains undiminished, I'm over conscious of the environment due to the prevalent thinking here, which has scared away many a male, who genuinely love kids and young people from working with children and youngsters, hence you are likely to find more women than men in Britain teaching and working with youngsters in schools, colleges, churches, etc. Yet I must not fail to mention here that children, dogs and other animals were among the first set of creatures that welcomed me to Britain.

In those early days, I remember Francis and I were going to a place, I now know as King's Cross, and whilst we were on the platform waiting to catch a train, a child was struggling to come to me, but the parents were resisting her with commuters on the platform watching the drama. She remained dogged in her determination and ran to hug me. I lifted her up on the platform to the admiration of the onlookers and she then peacefully leaned on my shoulder with the parents looking. I afterwards handed her over to her parents who were very pleased and full of gratitude and blessedness, waving the baby a blessed and memorable goodbye. Soon afterwards, Francis who was joyously beaming with laughter and blessedness at the whole pleasant drama between the kid and the parents trying to prevent her from coming to me, alongside other commuters began to ask me, "Do you know the kid?" And "No," was my reply, letting them to know I was new in the country but added, "I'm a Child Evangelist."

With respect to dogs, when I was new in the country, wherever I was on the bus and there was a dog, they would leave their owner to come to me feeling blessed as they wagged their tail and rubbed their body against mine.

However, I must confess, initially I did not like it and would shout asking the owners to call their dogs, be in control of, and not let them wander about scaring people on the bus, more so, they could bite passengers. But in the course of protesting to the owners, they together with the other passengers would say the dog had come to greet me.

During this time, I considered it an insult for the dogs' owners alongside others to say the dogs had come to greet me.

It took me years to buy into the idea of dogs going to greet a stranger, but now I'm used to the enthusiasm that dogs, cats and other creatures; including children and youngsters do often display whenever they see me, meet me in church and in public places.

One day, I was the only one at a bus stop in Manor House, waiting for a bus to go to Wood Green and a red squirrel which was perching on both trees and wall came down to where I was, picking up crumbs of food in between my legs unafraid. I was shocked and I then brought out my mobile phone and called a friend of mine, Taiwo Akinola, to tell him the mystery. Mr Akinola was not surprised in any least way, knowing me as an environmentalist/conservationist and a fighter for justice. He said, "You have been fighting to protect them. The squirrel knows you will not harm him, that is why he gets so close to you."

Also, the reader must be made aware too that the author as part of the extension of this ministry of his, has been involved since 2013 in professional mentoring at Post Graduate Level in City, University of London's Professional Mentoring Scheme (Postgraduate).

In fact, the City's Post Graduate Professional Mentoring Scheme kick-started with me as the first professional mentor of its PG Professional Mentoring Scheme, with a Nigerian lady as my mentee and she happened to be the first mentee on the PG Professional Mentoring Scheme of City.

That relationship blossomed to a point, where I was to later become a 'member' of their family, getting to know her mum, Dad, her elder sister and her husband; her other siblings – half brothers/sisters and members of her extended families – maternal and paternal!

But why this bond between me and children, youngsters, other creatures and all the 'least of these ones' of the Earth?

People have said to me variously, thus, "You have a good spirit."

"You have a gentle spirit."

"John is a holy man."

"Because you are always smiling."

"John is a great soul."

"John is very friendly."

"You are an avatar."

"You are a mystic."

"John is always in a good mood." And a Chinese customer of a major supermarket would often say to me, "You, happy, happy every time…happy; happy every time…every time happy, happy…why…how(?)" and he would add, whilst hugging me, "You, God me…You, God me." But I usually say an emphatic "No" to this, stoutly rejecting this notion of his because only God is God, and He alone can be God and no other – and God alone as the God of all of His creations – visible and invisible, animate and inanimate!

But in this project, I would announce to the reader that, "It is for these that I have come."

It must also be stated here that as an extension of this ministry into my academic enterprises, when it came to choosing a topic for my long essay in 2004, leading to my thesis at City, I carried out a research into the vexed topic of internet child abuse titled: *Is the Internet Becoming Much More Dangerous to Children?*

As the reader would have now known, my interest in children and youngsters can be categorised into the divine, which as I have said I cannot explain why, except that I know it is a ministry entrusted to me from above.

Therefore, it is only God Himself who knows why He has entrusted me with this gifting ministry as my life's work, and it is only He that will help me to accomplish it.

The second reason as I said is earthly – on the earthly plane – so I'm aware of it, and undoubtedly am able to explain to the reader based on the fact that when/ever I see babies/kids/children and youngsters, it's like beholding the face of the Almighty God – their innocence, serenity, seeming unblemishness, the love on their faces, the halos around their foreheads, particularly babies/infants – their smiles, the unspeakable atmosphere of peace in and around them, the total community amongst them and the harmonious peaceful coexistence of their world, unaffected, untroubled by the worries and anxieties of life which do often cripple the adults' lives and brought wrinkles upon their faces.

They relate with one another in an admirable, total and enviable camaraderie, with little or no fight, friction, conflict, quarrel and whenever there's one, they quickly forget, forgive and come back together to play together again.

What a beautiful world!

What a marvellous world! What a glorious world! What a wonderful world – the world of little children/infants! No wonder, Jesus said, "…for of such is the kingdom of God." – Luke 18:16.

However, anytime I see them in this elysian state where colour, creed, faith, philosophy, gender and sex do not matter, I have always been full of fear, lamenting that soon and very soon, society will pollute them as they grow up, poisoning their minds against one another, emphasising these differences and all the – *isms* – and ideologies that there are in our polluted, contaminated, scattered, racist, segregated, divided and bigoted world!

And having become contaminated/polluted, they (then) turn into beasts, monsters and ogres to devour the very society that has so corrupted them.

It is, therefore, the onus of this book to restore order in them and in their world and to return them to humanity and godliness in order to help them build a world without stain, corruption, a world of universal brotherhood, universal altruism, peace and justice, celebrating the oneness of our humanity, whilst yet here on earth.

A Reminder to My Young Friend

My dear friend,

How are ya?

Of late I have been in grief, tears, pain and sorrow over what I have been hearing about you in the media and from everybody regarding your now commonplace bestiality and monstrosity, which methinks you should not for any reason whatsoever be associated with.

Having pondered over the now endemic stabbings, killings and pervasive violence in the nation's cities which I'm told you now do regale with, it looks to me that you have put down your crown and forgotten your noble origin and birth as a citizen of eternity, hence you and others have turned the city to a wild, where the cubs are not allowed to grow up to become lions, the jungle where calves are not allowed to grow up to become elephants, the rainforest where the acorns are not allowed to grow up to become oaks and the pond, where the tadpoles are hindered from becoming frogs.

This, therefore, is my letter to you, my dear friend, to remind you of your noble origin and birth and to let you know that as a prince, princess, king and a queen you ought not to have sunk so low as to be stabbing, shooting, killing and maiming people and going ahead to steal and destroy their properties for which they have laboured.

At this juncture, with tears cascading down my cheeks about this bad news I have heard about you, I urge you as your dear friend and in the name of that umbilical cord that binds you and me together as citizens of this our great country and as members of one human family, take up your crown once more, and wear it in that characteristic and traditional nobility of yours, then retrace your steps and come to your senses.

And having reclaimed your sanity, I beg you in the name of the Governor of the universe to embrace and practice universal altruism and…

1. Stop stabbing people because when you do, you are the first to die, and by your action, you bring sorrow and anguish to homes and the nation.
2. Stop killing people, for only God can take life.
3. Stop hanging around in public places doing nothing, for you do often scare people to death by your presence, especially when in a group.
4. Don't intentionally block public roads, paths, alleys and entrances to your local supermarkets just to wind-up security officers and the police or just for the pleasure of it.
5. Don't ride your bike without a helmet, and don't ever ride your bike crisscrossing in a busy road, just to show-off, for many youngsters have lost their lives through this and got themselves unnecessarily maimed for life.
6. Never, never ever, be idle because the devil usually finds work for an idle youth. He might even recruit

you to do a very dirty, cruel and wicked job for him which will lead you to regret and be unhappy for life.
7. Don't waste your time, invest it!
8. Don't bury your talent – it is not true to say you haven't got at least a talent.
9. Get a life, plan your life, and live a planned and an organised life.
10. Get education because education is empowerment, and you can equally be empowered by learning a trade as formal or university education is not the only pathway of life.
11. Get a future, invest in your future.
12. Dare to dream and dream big or don't dream at all.
13. Always be focussed and be constant to your purpose.
14. You are not just passing through this world, but you are here for a grand purpose.
15. Never think the future is today. The future is, in fact, now!
16. Don't vandalise things.
17. Don't join bad company.
18. Don't let anyone disrespect you because you are a youth.
19. Don't join or belong to a gang, lest you might end up getting killed.
20. Don't let down your parents by your actions or inactions.
21. Don't listen to anyone who says you are not good enough, but take on board Martin Luther King's mother's advice to young Martin when he was just aged five, "You are as good as anyone else."

22. Speak out! Let your parents, loved ones, mentors, friends, authorities and the police know about all your fears, frustrations, worries, anxieties, concerns and all that threaten your life.
23. Never ever think of committing suicide or homicide for any reason whatsoever – no matter how hard your challenges and trials are.
24. Don't give up on life but keep on keeping on, for life is not a bed of roses. And remember, no cross, no crown.
25. Early to bed, early to rise.
26. Always plan your day by cultivating the notebook habit and have all your to-do list for each day thereon.
27. There's never a time that life's gonna be easy. In fact, in the coming age, it will be harder still, but keep on knocking, until the door is opened for you, and keep on searching until you find.
28. Don't smoke having your uniform on and it is my candid advice to you to keep off smoking.
29. Don't do crime or be involved in a crime, for the consequences are very grave – and never live a life of crime, for its scars are forever, even if you are forgiven by the state.
30. Don't ever bleach off your natural skin, for there is no such thing as a superior skin colour. It's all politics by the rabid racists to take undue advantage of the peoples of other cultures in order to grow their health and beauty industries.
31. Don't for the sake of making your friends/peers to laugh, scream all over the place in public places, especially in your local supermarkets and

convenience stores, kebabs, cafes, internet cafes, libraries, etc.

32. Don't fly-tip in and around your local supermarkets, especially at entrances, exits and car parks, lest you fly-tip into customers going in and out of the store or get knocked down by customers looking for places to park or by drivers trying to leave the car park.
33. Don't bring babies into the world when you are not ready, or just for the fun of it; for babies are not teddy bears or toys.
34. Don't do evil.
35. Always do what is right because it is right.
36. Aim at doing the first thing first – in other words, prioritise.
37. Absentee-fatherism is both an offence to humanity and God. If you cannot be there for your children, then stop bringing them into the world only to turn human cities into jungles full of predators. This ugliness and shame had its roots in slavery, and it has got to stop. And stop it must!
38. Never indulge in 'accompany'. It is simply gross irresponsibility.
39. "Train up your child the way they should go and when they grow up, there will not depart from it."

     – Proverbs 22:6

40. Babies of school-going age bringing children into the world is bad enough. Worse; baby mothers need parenting, and there's none. So, who then parents the baby mother's baby?
41. Don't borrow money to fund a lavish lifestyle.

42. Still, never ever borrow money to buy the latest and the trendy but borrow money to invest and educate your children.
43. O' Britain, has thou thyself practised British values?
44. O' Britain, thou need to apply the Rotary Four-Way test in dealing with all thy children.
45. O' Britain, has thou indeed, created a level playing field for all thy children?
46. O' Britain, love all thy children as thyself – and equally too, again I say, "Equally."
47. Don't be a problem but be the solution in your little corner and community.
48. Don't be a bad youth, but be an example of a good youth, a good citizen and a good patriot in word and in deed, building your nation from your little corner and community.
49. Volunteer your time and services to your community and local charity.
50. Read to improve yourself, for as Francis Bacon says, "Reading maketh a full man." In this wise, I say, "Reading maketh a youth."
51. Avail yourself the opportunities for learning as offered by your local learning centres – universities, libraries, computer centres, colleges and in all of these centres there abound free courses sponsored by the government, the EU, organisations and institutions.
52. Don't do play fighting on the streets, lest you might run into members of the public on their legitimate businesses, and you could get knocked down by moving vehicles.

53. Be a beacon of hope in the world and never do or plan evil against people, other creatures, things and society.
54. Be a change agent in the world – and according to Mahatma Gandhi, the very change that you want to see in the world.
55. Don't oppose, obstruct or antagonise the police who are out there on the streets doing their legitimate duties to keep all of us safe.
56. Don't hate or disrespect the police for doing their legitimate duty of keeping all of us safe.
57. Cooperate with the police and answer every of their questions if they are having a friendly conversation with you regarding any matter of interest to them, the public and the nation. In fact, all their works are for our sakes.
58. Also, let it be borne in mind that when the police don't sleep, when they abandon their families, so to say, to work in the most dangerous circumstances, risking their lives, deny themselves food and sleep, again, it is all for our sakes. But how much money as salary can really, really and actually compensate them for all their sacrifices on our behalf, on behalf of the nation and on behalf of posterity? Think, think, again I say, "Think!"
59. Never use racist word on anyone. Never ever!
60. Respect yourself, respect your parents, teachers, the police, others and all those in authority.
61. Never be a racist.
62. Never purpose in your heart to deliberately break the laws of the land just to make your friends, peer group

have a good laugh for the sake of it, and yourself feeling good, cool and high about your supposed bravely and boldness in breaking the laws.

63. Don't do drugs or take any substance that will make or keep you high, for their short, medium – and long – term, consequences are very grave.
64. In life, never ever, never, never take a short cut.
65. Don't take advantage of the poor 'the least of these ones' and those that are generally disadvantaged.
66. You shall not attend any party in which more than 5–10 guests who are all teenagers have been invited, except the organisers have planned to have security officers therein. Better any party such as a birthday party that will have more than ten teenagers as guests be held in a pub, where safety and security will not be compromised.
67. Don't take advantage of, or exploit persons of other races, assuming very erroneously that they don't know their rights or are here illegally. Let the appropriate authorities deal with all cases of immigration and don't ever take the laws into your hands.
68. Rest and then do your homework after school. Don't delay it till the last minute, for delay is dangerous.
69. Never procrastinate in life, for the old man procrastination is prowling about to steal your time.
70. Don't grow up without responsibilities. Help at home and involve yourself in doing home chores.
71. Don't smoke – moreover, don't smoke having your school uniform on.

72. Avoid arguments that will lead to a quarrel, fight or stabbing.
73. Don't be jealous/envious/bitter of/against your friends, brothers, sisters and other loved ones who you think are making faster progress than you in life, concluding they have left you behind. Bear in mind that your time too will come and it's coming sooner than you expected.
74. Always bear in mind that you are on your own life's journey with the spirit of your Maker leading you and not in a competition with anyone. If everyone around you has written you off and have erroneously concluded that you are a failure, just let them know very politely, "My time will come one day!" And I add, come sooner, it will. Just keep on, never giving up and never giving up on life.
75. Don't rush life, lest life will rush you. I'm called in my church, 'Brother no hurry in life'. What a beautiful name! I love that.
76. Write this message of life on the tablet of your heart, live fast, die young. Therefore, make haste slowly. One of life's best mottoes is, 'slow and steady wins the race'.
77. Don't start a family at a time you are supposed to be thinking of your education and the future.
78. Don't steal.
79. Don't nick
80. Don't lie – and don't ever lie against anyone.
81. Never bear false witness against your friends or neighbours.
82. Believe in yourself and be true to yourself.

83. Be self-reliant.
84. Purpose in your heart to be an honest, a trustworthy and a principled person.
85. It's all about brain and not brawn. Therefore, don't do violence to prove a point or go pumping up your body in the name of body building. It's just a sign of psychological inadequacy – 'inferiority complex', pure and simple!
86. Help others and help those who are in need, in your little corners.
87. Start to move the world from your little corner.
88. "Know yourself" – an ancient Egyptian (African) command to neophytes written on temples: "Man Know Thyself" which across centuries has erroneously been attributed to Socrates.
89. Fill your mind always with serious things.
90. Don't nick things at your local supermarkets or convenience stores.
91. Never forget that a sound mind is only to be found in a sound body.
92. Whenever you are in a group – your peer group or any, don't be too forward and don't be over inquisitive, for the inquisitive monkey always gets the active bullet.
93. If it's meant to be, it sure will be and there's nothing you can do about it. So, sing, 'Que Será, Será (Whatever Will Be, Will Be)' and move on.
94. Higher! Higher! Again, I say: "Higher!"
95. To the racist, I ask: "What do you see in others?" To you whose heart is full of hatred and bitterness such that you are now plotting to go and bomb places, stab,

kill, steal, maim and destroy, I ask, "What do you see in others?" To all who have been grooming young girls and boys for sex, I ask, "What do you see in others?" To you now on your way to go and stab, kill, burgle a fellow human being like yourself, I ask, "What do you see in others?"

96. *Mens sana in corpore sano* – 'A sound mind in a sound body.'

97. Never ever say to anyone, 'go to where you belong' just because you think such a person is not a member of your race or think they do not belong to your class or status.

98. *Nemo potest dare quod non habet* – 'You can't give what you do not have.' Each of us will give to the world, their communities and neighbours what they have on their inside. If you have love in your heart, you sure will give love, and correspondingly, if you have hatred on the inside of you, you will undoubtedly give hatred. Therefore, all racists, first and foremost, hate themselves hence their hatred for humanity, especially all those who are not members of their race.

99. It is not a bad thing or a shameful or an embarrassing thing to fail in a venture again and again because failure not only teach success, but it is success turned inside out. Therefore, I say to you boy, I say to you girl, "Fail, fail and fail and then go on to succeed, succeed and succeed *Ad infinitum* after your sinews had been strengthened through many failures."

100. My school principal, Mrs O. A. Alabi used to say to us during every Assembly at Aladura Comprehensive High School, Anthony Village, Lagos, Nigeria:
    - "Do a little at time."
    - "Your classroom is your office"
    - "A step at a time."
101. There's room for improvement, and always one at the top. See you at the top then!
102. Health is wealth.
103. Don't participate in modern slavery because it is a sin against God and all of humanity. Therefore, join the anti-slavery vanguard and report every case to the police.
104. Who goes a borrowing, goes a sorrowing.
105. You are in the library to read and not to make noise. The library is not a place you can run up and down screaming or play fighting, but indeed, a place to read, hence it is called the learning centre!
106. Don't be vindictive – always seeking to avenge wrong.
107. Don't be obsessed by other people's accents because their tongues are not primarily designed to speak English, but their own mother tongues, say Yala, spoken in Cross River, state of Nigeria.
108. Punctuality is the soul of business.
109. Honesty is the best policy.
110. Work, work and work! In all that you do – work, but work and rest, rest and work.
111. Be friendly, be kind.
112. Don't be an intolerant person – love, love and again I say, "Love and be considerate of others."

113. Be angry, but don't be bitter, lest it leads you to kill someone. Also, whenever you are angry, don't let it prolong, lest it leads to bitterness and hatred which may lead you to extreme incidents. So, let your anger be short-lived.
114. There must be no idle moment in all of your life's schedules.
115. Don't do crimes nor do silly things.
116. Never apologise for who you are or for your background, nor deprecate yourself by squeezing yourself into a class, where you make it a constant reference or refrain in any conversation. Be proud of who you are and your background.
117. Believe in yourself.
118. Appreciate yourself.
119. Celebrate you (yourself).
120. Give yourself a treat whenever you accomplish anything worthwhile.
121. Support a worthy cause.
122. Don't let the social or the conventional media rule your life. Take control of your life.
123. Don't be shifty – be a principled person. Let your yes be yes, and your no, no.
124. Don't bully anyone, and don't let anyone bully you because you are a youth. Remember, bullying is a crime.
125. Don't constitute a nuisance in your little corner or in public places.
126. Don't drink, don't smoke. But if you must drink, then drink very responsibly and never drink and get drunk or do binge drinking or enter a drinking

competition because some people before you have done that and died in the course of such irresponsibility.

127. Good youth don't use F-language or foul language.
128. Don't lose your head in the crowd.
129. Whenever you step out of your house, see yourself as an ambassador of your home, for you are the mirror by which your home, family and your type of upbringing and background reflect.
130. Go home straight after school hours or if you would like to stop at a nearby local shop to buy one or two things, proceed home thereafter immediately. Don't just be moving up and down for the sake of it in your school uniform, constituting public nuisance. Remember, you will have to do your homework to submit the next day.
131. Whenever you select items at your local supermarket store and go to the self-service checkouts, don't play smart by hiding some items and paying for just a few, hoping to exit without paying for the rest items. Therefore, ensure you pay for all the items you have selected. If you try to be stupid, the consequences are very severe as not only the CCTV is recording you, there are security officers, including under cover store detectives who are monitoring and keeping an eye on you.
132. Don't offer to become a drug mule/courier for anyone or any group of drug traffickers/peddlers. And don't let anyone or group of persons encourage/induce/entice or force you to be a drug mule for them, even if it is just one or a few time/s,

or just to go and buy drugs for anyone who is into drugs.

133. Don't just pass by your local libraries all the time without using them. Go inside and register as a member in order for you to borrow books therefrom. Also, whilst you are in your local library, don't turn yourself into a weaver bird or a canary, making a hell of noise, disturbing other library users.

134. Don't forget, your local library/learning centre is not a place you can hang out/around constituting a nuisance and making troubles.

135. Don't ever, ever take the laws into your hands.

136. Don't react to any violent social media challenge thrown at you by anyone or group of youth/yobs, but report this to the police after you have informed your parents/guardians about the incident.

137. Don't join bad company and never join a gang or belong to one – you are bound to end up in prison if caught, or have your life shortened if you get killed and so will not be able to fulfil your dreams, ambitions and aspirations in life any more.

138. Never ever leave your future behind you. Always carry your future with you wherever you go.

139. Remember, party time is not fighting time, nor is it a time to drink and get drunk and start misbehaving all over the place.

140. Whenever you want to organise any sort of legally acceptable party in your house or in your neighbourhood, ensure there are at least two older people in the house or within easy reach who will proactively diffuse any likely tension, or do hire a

security officer to man the party and the immediate vicinity to ward off any likely intruders/gate crashers posing for a fight.

141. Don't spike people's drinks at parties or in pubs or anywhere else, for spiking is a very serious crime, and if caught, the end will not be pleasant for you and your entire future.

142. Always be positive, no matter what. Look on the bright side of life. Keep out pessimism from your life, be positive and enthusiastic always.

143. Never be negative but do well to cultivate the spirit of positive mental attitude (PMA) and the spirit of possibility thinking.

144. Never be weighed down by momentary trials, for these too shall pass away just like the others, for they are just mere waters under the bridge.

145. Never remake yourself to please others, especially the advertisers and other mercantile predators, but you must accept and appreciate who you are – beautifully and wonderfully made, for from birth there is an eternal signature of 'good' stamped on you by your Maker/Creator. Therefore, don't apologise for being you (for who you are), remain unapologetically you! So be the unapologetic you and let me be the unapologetic me and let them be the unapologetic them!

146. When a person of other race/culture does not fit into your stereotypical prism because they have resolved to assert themselves and their rights to prevent you from exploiting or taking advantage of them, don't resort to your usual racist tantrum of name calling

and character assassination such as 'they are rude', 'disrespectful', 'aggressive', 'not friendly', 'violent', 'weird', 'cheeky', 'dodgy', 'not helpful' or making such ridiculous statement that they have strong accent. Also, don't start mounting uncalled for propaganda against them, just for the simple reason that they disagree with or offend you, for this type of attitude simply shows you as a person who is grossly immature and full of hatred first for yourself and the whole of humanity, and not just for the person that has disagreed with you or offended you.

147. Do well to cultivate the habit of self-restraint/self-control because life's golden motto is, 'nothing in excess'.

148. The time of youth is the golden age of your life, but whilst you bask in its effulgent glory, never fail to make haste whilst the sun shines.

149. Always look before you leap. Also, never fail to think before you act, for some silly youth that do act before they think have all got drowned in the fathomless ocean of life.

150. Wealth gotten without working for it (www: ill-gotten wealth) or without labouring for it will cause you endless sorrow, for untold tragedies are embedded in such 'wealth' acquired without sweating – without working for it.

151. Larger! Larger! Larger!

152. Always nourish your mind by reading great books which abound in your local learning centre/library.

153. Always engage yourself in a great, uplifting, inspiring and healthy conversation because by doing so, you will keep your mind flooded and saturated with serious and excellent things.

154. Never aim to put yourself in a family way just because you want to get a council flat, for the pains, sadness and sorrow that come with such greed, selfishness and an unplanned life are very grievous to bear and you may end up getting crushed by their unparalleled weightiness throughout the whole of your life – and you don't want to live in the same house with your son as your 'husband' for life, or if the product of that often so-called 'error' is a woman, as your female 'partner' for the rest of your life.

155. Up your ambition beyond just having a pair of trainers, a flat screen television, and beyond even owning a car and living in a rented flat or a studio flat, for all these are mere toys and properties. Therefore, go for the grandest and highest values of life.

156. Treat all with respect, especially as you would want them to treat you.

157. 'Be not proud!' Whatever be your achievements and glory, be not proud, pompous and haughty, but be humble, for pride goes before a fall or destruction.

158. Don't be a spendthrift, but learn to cultivate the habit of saving, frugality and investment.

159. Don't ever try to live above your means, for you will live to regret it.

160. Don't gossip and never be a gossiper, for you will end up isolating yourself and lose the trust, cordiality and friendship of all.
161. Don't bring children into the world for the taxpayer to feed and train, do so only when you are truly ready and are able to fend for and train them by giving them all the necessities of life.
162. Don't ever threaten people by saying "I will kill you and nobody will ask me" or "I will smash your head and nothing will happen".
163. Honesty is still the best policy – love it, cuddle it, cultivate the habit of being honest and practise honesty always.
164. Don't go about impregnating girls all over the place as if all there is in the world is to 'conquer' girls at your pleasure, leaving the problems to society to bear the burden of your uncontrolled lasciviousness.
165. The absence of a father figure or the so-called role model in your upbringing and in your life generally must not make you to go about with a heart full of uncontrolled anger and hatred for society as this may lead you to kill and spend the rest of your life in jail.
166. If you are naturally hot-tempered, seek help from experts and enlist yourself in an anger management programmes that abound in the country.
167. Do something for yourself and about your life generally. Stop moaning every time because you are from a poor background or a highly deprived community, so you can't further your education. This is a lie and a defeatist attitude! Britain is a land

of limitless opportunities. You can get loan/bursary to further your education. Moreover, all colleges/universities and learning centres/libraries in the country offer free short courses and you can avail yourself of these opportunities that abound. Also, most companies in the UK offer training and development programmes for their staff for purpose of career progression within the establishment. What is more, apprenticeship programmes abound in Britain. So, stop wasting your time complaining. Again I say, "Do something for yourself and about your future. You better get up and go or perish like a fool."

168. There is grandeur in simplicity.
169. Don't turn the divine act of bringing babies into the world to a factory mass or over producing to destroy other markets.
170. You say, "I have given babies to Daniella, to Kimberly, to Shanna, Shanelle, to Amelia, to Natalie, etc, etc!" But what sort of a life is this? What's there to be proud of this type of gross irresponsibility and purposeless wickedness, except it be a display of folly in the eyes of responsible, disciplined, conscientious humanity and a sin against God. So, what sort of a person are you then, if you go about breeding without feeding, without training, but at the expense of the taxpayer? Therefore, bear in mind that, 'Whatever a person sows that they shall reap.'
171. You say babies are not toys. But this is exactly what you have turned them into – mere toys being

dragged about all over the place on buggies in such ugliness!

172. Face the future with hope and optimism. Challenges will always come your way in life, and there is nothing you can do about this reality as 'no cross, no crown'.

173. I can, and I will. I can, and I will.

174. About your marriage: Marry a person that is of age, mature, ready; financially, socially, psychologically, sociologically and ready to shoulder every responsibility that comes with family life. So, don't let your chocolate turn into vinegar or sour grapes.

175. If you don't respect yourself, there is not a person on the planet Earth that you will ever respect and, consequently, there is no one on the planet Earth that will respect you.

176. Heaven loves a smartly dressed youth.

177. Be content with what you have.

178. Never be satisfied with your achievements and don't become pompous because of your achievements.

179. No human child is a monster, except the society by design turns them into, and unless the child themselves gets themselves choked up by the weeds and tares of life by mixing their honey with sour grapes.

180. If you want to be a grown-up person, nature will start feeding you with 'stones', 'rocks' and 'bones' after your teen years, whereupon you had enjoyed a lot of 'milk' and 'chocolates' – although some of

you were fed with 'boulders', 'rocks' and 'bones' even before you were formed in the wombs.

181. Always be on your guard because people, even your loved ones and friends, will start pulling you down through petty jealousy and envy, especially when they realise you are a talented person, excelling more than them, and when they know you are going somewhere or making some headway in life.

182. Believe in yourself and believe in God.

183. Be diligent, for the heavens do support, promote and advance any person diligent in their work.

184. Be hygienic!

185. Don't spit in public places.

186. Don't throw your rubbish indiscriminately in the public. Consider the environmental/hygiene (cleaners) officers who day by day keep our environment and cities clean so that we do not fall sick through catching germs/diseases.

187. Always wash your hands whenever you come to the house from wherever you have been to during the day.

188. Always wash your fruits before eating them.

189. Make sure you wash your hands whenever you use private or public convenience room/bathroom.

190. Stop lying. A person of honour and integrity will never ever lie. Tell the truth and shame the devil.

191. Stop! Don't rush.

192. Health is wealth – look after yourself and your soul.

193. Learn to punctuate your life as often as you can. If you cannot put a comma in your life, once in a

while, put a semicolon at least in your life some of the time.

194. Have a personal moderator and a mentor as you would have a personal trainer; someone who can call you back when you are making a wrong move in life, someone who can look at you straight in the eye and say to you, "On this occasion, you are wrong," without you taking an offence.

195. Labour, again I say, "Labour, labour and wait patiently for the time of harvest."

196. "Success awaits whoever labours," was my motto at Aladura Comprehensive High School, Anthony Village, Lagos, Nigeria.

197. Show me your friends and I will tell you who you are. Ensure you have good friends who are going somewhere in life, dreaming big dreams that will make them attain their life's great goals, and not those that will lead you into troubles and wreck your life's voyage.

198. During the Halloween festival celebration, aim to enjoy yourself by having fun with your rollicking friends, but don't intentionally plan to injure people for the fun of it – pelting people with eggs and throwing fireworks at others, the police and moving vehicles or into your local supermarket stores. Also, ensure you and your friends do not gather in and around your local supermarkets, intimidating customers, blocking entrances and exits of your local supermarkets and by so doing, preventing customers from going in and out. Whenever you indulge in all of these bad behaviours just to feel

cool and high and make your friends to laugh and cackle foolishly, you are endangering people's lives and making your local supermarket stores shut early, for this is a huge loss to your local supermarkets, and by this very uncouth behaviour of yours, not only that customers and staff will be trapped inside or injured, some people might even lose their jobs due to losses in sales for that day. Think! Think! Again, I say, "Think, and you are not too young to think!"

199. Procrastination is the thief of time.
200. Never bite the finger that has fed you. Be thankful, be grateful for any little kindness and help.
201. Hi girls! It is my candid advice that whenever you are approaching 19–21 years of age, you should begin to consider seriously transiting from your male peer group of the same age bracket, who probably were your former class/schoolmates or live in the same neighbourhood with you or those you met at college, but are not yet ready for family life. You, therefore, need to at this time make friends who are a few years older than you, say 25–30 plus, who may be thinking of starting a home/family, and who in the event of any often so-called 'mistake'/'error' will be able to shoulder the responsibility of fatherhood and family life at this time, especially if such young male adults are gainfully employed. Sticking to your old male class/college mates of your generation may lead to regrets, bitterness and all sorts of untowardness in the event of any so-called 'error'/'mistake',

resulting in a child, and in most cases you will be abandoned by the randy fella, and you could remain unmarried for life as most men generally like to start their family lives on a clean slate without carrying anyone's child into their homes. Think! Think! Think, for the consequences of not acting wisely are very, very grave, incalculable and often 'very' unpleasant. You may be 'rewarded' with a council flat, but you will soon realise that life is not all about having a council flat of your own at a school-going age. Lastly, don't allow yourself to be used by every irresponsible man that comes your way in life to give them children here and there, and all over the place – such as having three–seven children for three, five different men! You know, this is not life and it's very embarrassing and very shameful too.

202. Wider! Wider! Wider!

203. Don't succumb to the temptations, no matter how beneficial you are misled to think there will be to yourself, members of your family and your faith – any deities that cannot defend themselves are not worth having, and not worth worshipping!

204. People don't kill for God or on His behalf, but they kill out of their bestial inclination, beastly and predatory instinct and tendency, and such gruesomeness, cruelty and purposeless malignity is a testimony to the degradation of their souls. Although such people have a zeal for God, but not according to knowledge.

205. Don't let anyone who has gone to collect money from the East, recruit you to strap bombs on your

body to go and kill and kill for and on behalf of God. If God is indeed God, let Him fight for or defend Himself. As a matter of fact, no God needs you to fight for Him; no God needs you to kill for Him or on His behalf – and again I say, "If God be God – let Him defend Himself by fighting for Himself!" The God that cannot defend Himself and fight for Himself, such that He needs a human being to fight His wars and kill, maim, steal and destroy for Him and on His behalf is not worth the name God, and is not worth having and must be binned for His unparalleled weakness and cowardice. Therefore, my friend, after they have collected money from the East, and you are approached by any of those greedy, cowardly, selfish, very heartless and wicked people, just say to them very politely, G.D.I.Y (Go and do it yourself)! But what about their own children? Can their children not undertake to go on such an evil errand for and on behalf of this their so-called cowardly and very timid god?

206. Don't groom young girls for sex.
207. Don't exploit young girls or take advantage of their vulnerability, just because they are young.
208. Don't groom young girls to avenge what you think are historical wrongs their ancestors had done to your race and nations by killing, brutalizing and plundering their resources.
209. Don't sell colleagues' or customers' data entrusted to you by your company.

210. Always take responsibilities for your actions and inactions. It cannot be that all the time, it is people around you that are wrong, and not you for once.
211. What do you see in others?
212. Invest! Invest! Again I say, "Invest!"
213. Aim to succeed and be a huge success and an influence in the world.
214. Children, racism is wickedness and pure evil.
215. Don't spike people's drinks in pubs, at parties or anywhere else.
216. *Car pe diem* (Seize the day!).
217. Create your chance where you stand now or where you are now because no one will give you a chance.
218. Seek your standing place yourself and move the world.
219. Stop your incessant complaints, moaning, murmurings about your life now and your condition generally.
220. If you don't like your life now, recreate it, and you can also recreate yourself to think positively and creatively.
221. Don't be pessimistic, for it is spirit-weighing.
222. Look at the heavens – the moon is your past, the sun your now, and the stars are your unseen future.
223. If you are moving with friends that are sure going nowhere; and are always pessimistic about everything, and about every venture, situation and circumstances, and who for them nothing ever or will ever work/s, thinking things can never get better, but worse; then summon the courage to tell them very politely that they are not part of your

journey of life, or just exit or disembark from their old truck 'go-nowhere'.

224. Aspire! Again, I say to you today: "Aspire!"
225. Never ever, indulge in self-deprecation such as, "I'm completely useless", "I'm worthless", "I don't even know why I am here on this earth", etc.
226. Always talk up yourself and as often as possible, give yourself a pep talk.
227. You must always move with aspiring friends/peer group/s, self-motivated lots, optimistic people, self-starters, proactive and team playing lots.
228. If you don't like your life as it is now, change it. And if your present environment is not conducive for your growth, if it is not helping you to nurture and nourish your ambition/s, aspirations and vision/s, then relocate.
229. Endeavour to have a personal aims and objectives and a mission statement as if you were a business plan.
230. By the way, what is your life's master plan?
231. Have friends that will sharpen you, and friends that have lofty goals and ambitions, and not those that will pull you down whenever you want to make any move in life.
232. Be aware that friends that are permanently inflicted with PhD Syndrome (Pull him Down) will always seek to pull you down.
233. Never ever give up on life.
234. Again, change your environment if your environment is pulling you down. The only thing you cannot change in life are your natural parents

because the bond between you and them are both spiritual and biological.

235. Be you! Just be you and nobody else. Again I say, "Be you and don't apologise to anyone for being you, for you are you unapologetically."

236. Don't let anyone mess up your destiny, God-given purpose and true self.

237. Run away from negative people and do always cultivate the habit of positive mental attitude (PMA).

238. Up, boy! Up, girl! Smile, and again, I say, "Smile!"

239. When you wake up in the morning, greet all around you. And when you want to retire to bed at night, bid all around you, good night.

240. Don't carry your yesterday into today nor your today into your now.

241. Don't postpone that which you are supposed to do now but do it now – and now is the time!

242. Don't delay your homework. Do it now!

243. Mind your language.

244. Watch your mouth.

245. Mind your business.

246. Don't procrastinate because procrastination is the thief of time.

247. Don't live a double life, presenting to your parents 'the good child' you, but to the world, 'the bad child' you. In other words, you are good in the house/at home, but bad outside.

248. Don't ever mind the racists; there's no such a thing as a superior race, and there is no superior skin colour either or a superior culture, and civilisation.

All human beings the world over are equal before God, our Maker – and no upper, middle or lower/working classes.

249. You are not a monkey. Anyone who calls or refers to you as a monkey, majestically extend your hand of fellowship to them, but never fail to whisper into their ears thus, 'only a monkey doth recognises a monkey!'

250. You are not educationally subnormal. In fact, there must not be such a thing in any civilised body politic.

251. Your history does not start from slavery and don't let anyone so deceive you. Therefore, endeavour to find out about your true and actual roots.

252. Up your expectations about yourself, if people have low expectations of you.

253. Don't ever feel inferior to anyone or let anyone make you look inferior to them or allow anyone to make you develop inferiority complex in yourself.

254. Strive for excellence.

255. Master! Master! Master!

256. Don't let anyone mess up your destiny. Take control of your destiny, for you are its sole and only director and custodian, and not anyone else.

257. Don't nick!

258. Don't steal!

259. Don't cheat!

260. Don't rob!

261. Don't defraud!

262. Don't do money laundry!

263. But be a man of honour and integrity.

264. Don't be ashamed of your accent, for your accent was primarily designed to speak your native language/mother tongue.
265. Be confident.
266. Believe in yourself.
267. Be ready and willing to serve, rather than to be served. Aim to be the servant leader.
268. Don't throw your rubbish just anywhere on the street or in public places. Look for the nearest public bin and put them therein.
269. Don't gossip. And never gossip anyone.
270. No one can stop you in life. Only you can stop you in life.
271. Expect the good as well as the bad. That's what life is all about. Life is that, that is smooth and rough, rough and smooth.
272. Life has given you a lemon, make a lemonade out of it; life has given you a fish, turn that fish into a fishery; life has given you a loaf of bread, establish a bakery industry therefrom. More, life has given you at least a talent, don't bury it!
273. Be that good Samaritan on life's Jericho road.
274. Your kind of friends tells who you are.
275. Don't look down on anyone doing what you consider as common job because that is what they have got now to keep their bodies and souls together instead of going to steal. At least with this, they are not likely going to be a burden to the taxpayer.
276. Don't write off anyone, no matter the station of life you have met them. But why play God when you

don't know what the next moment holds for you, the 'judge'?

277. Don't be judgemental.
278. Don't do gang. And don't let anyone force you into joining one or give you a knife to go and fight members of the other gangs.
279. Hastily arrived, hastily crash-landed. Hastily acquired, hastily down the drain/lost/disappeared, and hastily gathered, hastily scattered!
280. If you are given everything you want by your parents, it means they don't love you and don't want you to grow and become a person of great worth in society.
281. Don't indulge in binge drinking. It is my candid advice to you to keep off drinking and smoking if you can. But if you must drink, then drink responsibly.
282. You are guilty of over generalisation if one member of a race offends you, annoys you or has defrauded somebody, or intentionally or unintentionally hurts or kills someone and you hastily generalise, "This is how all of them are."
283. Judging people by their colour and not by the content of their character is the worst exhibition of racial prejudice, cultural ethnocentrism and gross irresponsibility.
284. If you are always fond of mounting propaganda against a person of another race who you naturally dislike/hate, or in a disagreement with or actually have quarrelled with or who has offended you or whom you have offended, so that all around you –

your friends and work colleagues will for no just reason hate that person and begin to isolate them and treat them very unjustly/unfavourably, it then means you are a rabid racist, grossly immature, you revel in purposeless wickedness and a first class sadist who loves seeing your fellow human beings in an unhappy, sad and isolated state.

285. Believe in yourself. Believe!

286. Check yourself, if you do always revel in judging people by the colour of their skin or lapse into racial tantrum when you cannot stand an argument, it is either that you are sick in the mind and having a soul full of garbage/rubbish or you are out for a purposeless mischief for the pleasure of it.

287. Never ever plot to kill someone or pour acid on someone who has snatched your girlfriend or boyfriend or have wronged you in some other way.

288. If your boyfriend or girlfriend jilted you, try and try, and try to get them back. If your candid efforts to talk it over with them did not yield results, get your trusted mutual friends to speak to them on your behalf, and if these efforts again did not make them come back to you, give them a little bit of space during which time you may choose to try again or move on. If in the long run, you are unable to get them back, comfort yourself with the fact that there are many fishes in the ocean, who are prettier, more beautiful and more handsome! But never ever think of harming them or resort to doing them a permanent damage using a corrosive substance. And don't forget, you yourself are the first to be

damaged permanently because the law of the land will sure show you no mercy for your brutality, bestiality and monstrosity.
289. Don't abuse the confidence reposed in you by people, authorities and society.
290. Don't betray people, country, organisations and institutions for which you work because you will lose their confidence and trust if you do.
291. Be loyal, but don't be stupid!
292. Your breakthroughs shall come to you in any of these four seasons in the creation calendar:
- The set time.
- The appointed time or the time appointed.
- In the fullness of time.
- In the time of life.

So, stop troubling yourself unnecessarily!

293. Be hopeful!
294. Why be downcast because you couldn't get that job after a gruelling interview? Up, boy! Up, girl! Tomorrow is another day. What is more, there are more interviews coming.
295. Avoid stereotype and never judge people by the colour of their skin. But who then indeed has made you a judge over the people of other cultures and colours?
296. If a person is angry and raises their voice or speaks loudly, don't then begin to say they are aggressive and go about telling people so. There's nothing whatsoever that is wrong in people getting angry

and expressing themselves in a loud voice. You should bear in mind that people all over the world can be divided into, what I had come up with after reflecting upon these grave error of judgement as, expressive and inexpressive cultures. They are people from other cultures who naturally speak loudly, laugh loudly because they are full of life and vigour. And these often do reflect in their mannerisms and idiosyncrasies, whilst on the other hand, they are other people from other cultures who like to bottle up things, generally cold, sting like vipers and are generally economical in the way they express themselves. There's, therefore, nothing you can do about this. This is how God has created them to be, and never ever arrogantly embark on such a gargantuan self-appointed mission of trying to or wasting your time and deluding yourself you will 'civilise' them.

297. Be aware that people from expressive cultures gesticulates a lot, and whenever they do, respect such mannerism and don't lapse into your 'civilising mission' agenda and label them as aggressive, lying that they want to attack you.

298. Don't look at the world only from your own very narrow prism, lest you will be guilty of an error of judgement. There are over seven billion peoples in the world who all come from diverse cultures. Therefore, there's no such a thing as a superior culture, race or civilisation as cultural ethnocentrists often do like to delude, indulge, deceive themselves

and so draw up such an erroneous conclusion from their own very narrow prism.

299. The world is neither 'white' nor 'black' nor 'brown' nor any other 'colour', but just the 'world' our 'planet' as God has created it to be – so don't be guilty of any such cultural narrowness and arrogance. Come out of your cocoon, your cave, delusion, your hiding place, your shell and meet the world and all of its very sweet, wonderful and friendly peoples. Be you, therefore, tolerant and accommodating!

300. In life, it is not possible you have everything you need. If your parents give you everything you need, it means they are bringing you up to become a parasite. But if your parents do really want you to grow up and achieve a resounding success, let them give you a little of all that you will ever want them to provide you, and correspondingly a little of your needs and then leave you to go and do your own fishing in the deep ocean of life and plant your own acorn in the desert and find an oasis by yourself to water and nurture it to grow to become an oak.

301. Never ever be involved in moped crime or use vehicles/bikes/moped to commit crimes. It is unfair to forcefully snatch from people/passers-by what does not belong to you, and it's very dangerous to use such a method to commit a crime.

302. Flush your heart 24/7, and vacuum clean your mind 24/7 and always nourish your soul with positive and inspiring conversations. If your environment does not have the right 'manure' for your personal

growth and development, either recreate/change it or relocate to an environment that can help nourish your growth and advancement in order to become a huge success, a positive force in your nation and a global influencer.

303. Cultivate the habit of self-restraint. In other words, discipline yourself.
304. Don't chew the cud 24/7 because you are not a cow and you could become obese and become a burden to the taxpayer and the NHS.
305. Apply moral restraint and moderation in all that you do think, say and do.
306. Don't join Moped gang.
307. Child, in life never run someone's race by suddenly switching from your life's track or life's lane to theirs, lest you stumble and fall, and may die subsequently.
308. Also, don't live your life expecting to step into someone's shoes because your shoes are big enough, if not bigger.
309. Grow up!
310. Never ever gang rape a girl/boy or rape anyone yourself.
311. Stop! Don't feed on rubbish.
312. Don't drive if you are under-aged, as it is not only against the law – it can cost you your life.
313. You are not allowed by the law to buy alcohol as an underaged person nor are you to buy alcohol for anyone or send anyone to buy for you at your local supermarket.

314. Friend, I sometime think you have a canary or a weaver bird in your mouth. But why not be sober and be reflective for a moment?
315. Learn to tame your tongue because it is good to do so.
316. There is no such a thing as 'failure', but failure is a springboard to success.
317. The sky is not the limit, but the springboard and the beginning.
318. Learn to wait for your time.
319. And wait for your turn in a queue.
320. Do not try to do everything at once, but do a little at a time and take a step at a time.
321. You risk becoming obese when you indulge in eating 24/7 indiscriminately.
322. Cultivate the habit of saving and investing very early because it will do you good.
323. Don't talk above people.
324. Don't be a layabout.
325. Run life and don't ever let life run you.
326. Don't let the media and the advertisers run your life for you, telling you what to think, how to think, what to say, what to do, how to look, what to wear; to what size you should reduce yourself and other such nonsense as the perfect shape, size, perfect life, perfect beauty, perfect look, perfect living and perfect life.
327. Don't let the media reduce you to a robot, a puppet and a marionette at the pleasure of their ungovernable mercantile and commodification instinct.

328. Be yourself. Be who you want to be without having to apologise to anyone, and accept yourself just as you are, and appreciate you for being you, and learn to celebrate yourself. Above all, give thanks for the beautiful you.
329. Always keep hope alive no matter what.
330. Never trouble the pensioners or burgle them or talk to them disrespectfully because they have served the nation well and are now on retirement, so let them enjoy their retirement life and live in absolute peace.
331. Never live your life to please any person or perpetually seek people's approval or always look to be approved by people.
332. As you are about to begin your life's journey, I urge you to get the right and reliable satnav, so you don't end up at an unintended destination.
333. If you are from a broken home, don't use this as an excuse for lack of growth and progress in life, and don't ever carry about you the anger that might have arisen as a result of such a background and explode always at the slightest provocation. If you do, you will scare people away from you and no one will want to befriend a human volcano.
334. Whenever you are offended by anyone, never say, I have forgiven you, but I will not forget.
335. If you are a Condition-Able person (CAP-special needs), do not focus on your condition, but focus on your abilities, strength and your very bright future.
336. Do not listen to whatever people say about you, because whatever they say about you does not matter but what you think, say and do about

yourself. Accept yourself just as you are and celebrate you unapologetically.

337. Don't become overconfident or complacent if you are good in anything, especially if you are brilliant academically, or have expressed your talent early enough to be so celebrated or have become a celebrity.

338. Do not listen to the voice of an evil genius.

339. Be careful about listening to voices generally – learn to sift the good advice of such voices from the bad. It is also my candid advice that you discuss what you hear from the super sensible with a confidant or any very trusted persons – your parents, teachers, mentors, pastors, imams, etc.

340. Can I know why is it that whenever you are in an argument, or in a brawl or just have a disagreement with a person of another race, you turn round to mount propaganda against the person saying that they were rude, disrespectful, discourteous, aggressive and almost attacked you, especially if they gesticulated in the course of the argument? But when the same scenario plays out between you and someone of your race, you merely say that the person was angry with you or was unhappy with you or had ago at you. Do you then mean that anyone who is not of your race does not have emotions, even in the 21st century, whilst you recognise that the person of your race possesses emotions, hence have the right to be angry?

341. Don't be biased or prejudiced and engage in a double standard when dealing with people outside of your race.
342. Obey your school's/college's rules and regulations as well as your class's ground rules.
343. Child, be humble. Again, I say to you today: "Child, be humble."
344. Again, I say to you child, "Humble yourself and be gentle, for these virtues are good for your promotion and overall advancement."
345. Keep calm and move on, if your parents' marriage broke up after all else to get them to mend fences have failed. I know that this can be very painful, but never allow this to affect you to the point of changing the course of your life, consequent upon you deciding to change your entire destiny – moving from being a good child to a bad child. Thus, again, I say, "Keep calm and move on. Life goes on after all. All, all must be well."
346. Be the first to greet those older than you when you wake up in the morning. Don't stand staring at them expecting them to be the first to greet you. And in like manner, when you return from school, greet all those who are older than you – your parents, foster parents, your guardians and all your elders. Also, don't forget to close the day by bidding them "Good night" when you are about to retire to bed, for such a 'good night' may be the final you can ever say to them.
347. Do not forget to give thanks when you are about to go to bed, just as it is expected of you to give thanks

when you wake up in the morning, before setting out for your day's businesses.

348. Don't throw fireworks at the police, pedestrians and vehicles during the Guy Fawkes Night or at any other time because you could get people injured and maimed for life.

349. And don't hang around during this time at your local store, intentionally obstructing their customers, throwing stones, empty plastic bottles and all sorts of things at the glass window of your local store or into the store, for you might get people injured and deformed for life. Think! Think, and be considerate of others.

350. Learn how to cook at home and take turn to cook alongside your family members.

351. Don't take change from the 'coins out' of your local supermarket store and put them in your pocket or use them to buy things. That's stealing!

352. There's is no such thing as a perfect body, figure, statistics, size, etc. You are a masterpiece just as you are and a photocopy of yours does not exist anywhere in the world!

353. Don't let your life or how you look be decided by modelling agencies or the advertising agencies or the media generally.

354. Don't let yourself be deceived by any of these entities. You better love the beautiful you unapologetically and celebrate you (yourself) without having to apologise to anyone about you, for you are just you as simple as that!

355. When you go into the customer toilet of your local store to free yourself, ensure you do not splash/litter faeces all over the place, using faeces to do graffiti or use their tissue papers more than you need or roll them all over the place (floor).
356. If you don't have money on you, then don't go shopping, expecting other customers to pay for the goods/products you have selected, thereby using this tactic to delay the queue at your local supermarket store or go nicking. You must discipline yourself in this regard and in all aspects of your life.
357. Don't always walk or go about as a victim or with a victim mentality, whereupon you will in any disagreeable circumstance resort to asking: "Is it because I'm white?", "Is it because I'm Asian?" or "Is it because I'm black?"
358. Whenever you are in your local supermarket, especially after school hours or in a group of other youngsters, don't ever kick products that fell on the floor about irresponsibly as if you were kicking a football at your local football field in order to make your peers have a good but obviously stupid laugh, or keep kicking the products about to the cheering and yelling of your friends or picking products from the floor, lifting them up and hitting them on the floor again and again for the packaging to get torn/burst with their contents falling down on the floor and scattering all over the place just to again, make your friends cackle, giggle, laugh and roll on the floor. This type of behaviour is nothing but gross

indiscipline, sheer wickedness and crass stupidity. And no young person with a good parenting and from a good home will do such a thing. Remember, having your uniform on, makes you an automatic ambassador of your school/college and your home. Also, don't hop onto the shopping trolley so your friends can push you around the shop floor, getting in the way of customers and obstructing their shopping, nor should you hop on top of a pallet and be riding it about the shop floor, nor be pushing the shopping basket all over the shop floor, nor push the giant cages with products inside them all over the shop floor just to make your friends/peer group laugh very foolishly about the place on the shop floor. These are very bad habits which do put customers and onlookers off. Don't forget, you are the mirror of your family, home and the type of upbringing you have had from your parent/s.

359. Whilst working on the street, roadside or whilst you are in your local supermarket store, never ever jump up and touch or hit the head of a bald person or touch/hit the head of any elderly person/security officer, no matter how lightly just to make your friends reel on the floor with laughter.

360. Whenever you go to your local supermarket store, don't sit on the bagging area or empty baskets area or try to force open the self-service check out's till safe.

361. Don't also, push the trolleys about on the shop floor of your local supermarket store, with your friends jumping inside them or for your friends to push

them around the shop floor for others to yell, yell, laugh and laugh. Be disciplined!

362. Arrive early to all your appointments and stop giving excuses upon excuses, especially when you have purposed to make it a habit, to always arrive late.

363. Don't ride your bike into your local supermarket store. And don't ride your bike around, whilst you are in your local supermarket store. Apart from this behaviour being a bad habit, you could get shoppers knocked down and deform them for life.

364. Don't use your bike to block the entrance/exit of your local supermarket or convenience store or leave your scooter right in the middle of the entrance of your local supermarket or convenience store.

365. Always remember the child of who you are.

366. Let this be your life's pledge henceforth, "I will humble myself and I will always endeavour to live a life of humility as possible as I can!"

367. Allow the constant flow of love from the highest to lubricate your heart like the olive oil and spread this love to all that come your way in life, and to the world entire, nay, the whole of humanity.

368. Don't expect things to always go your way, for such is not life. Life is all about compromises, a sort of give and take.

369. If you always do get annoyed easily, it is either that you are naturally temperamental, or you have a fragile ego in which case, you must do something

about it. Discipline yourself to be less sensitive/eruptive or go for anger management.
370. Unless a guide dog, don't go into your local supermarket or convenience store with your puppy or a dog.
371. Avoid watching violent films if you can. But if you must, never make it a habit, lest you may get addicted to it and this could blur your world of reality and there is a likely tendency that you might end up living in a world of fiction when dealing with situations of reality!
372. When you are faced with diverse trials or challenges, count your blessings and name them one by one. If unpleasant circumstances or situations, rise to them and stay on top; be bold, be strong and hold strong, be stoical, smile in the midst of such a storm until you get on top and overcome.
373. Don't talk to strangers. Be security and safety conscious.
374. Don't accept an invitation for an outing from a person you don't know or just meet online. Let your parents/guardians or the police know about this.
375. When you have known/regular visitors/guests in your house, especially people very well known to the entire family members such as members of your extended family, family friends, church, mosque members, make them feel welcome.
376. Don't always assume that those who are not members of your race are stupid, uncivilised and uncivil and don't know their rights.

377. They who will live life well and live it to the fullest must learn to punctuate their lives on daily basis.
378. Don't always think that in all things and in all circumstances, it is the members of the other races that are wrong, can do bad or do bad things, whereas, you delude yourself always into thinking that members of your race, including yourself can never ever do wrong, do bad, or do bad things or be wrong.
379. The world is neither red, orange, yellow, green, blue, brown, black, violet, purple, white nor dark. It is just the world created as it is with all its imperfections and all of its diverse peoples and cultures.
380. When you go shopping at your local shop, don't go disturbing the security officers that are there to keep everybody safe for the fun of it. You are not also there as a judge of the security officers' mood and character, screaming out to them as if they are robots having batteries inside them, "Smile! Smile! Why aren't you smiling? You look like the unhappiest person in the world. You are particularly not a happy person. You look like you don't like your job. You are the saddest person on Earth." You better mind your shopping. You are in your local supermarket to shop; to do your shopping and not to seek attention, approval or acknowledgement from anyone, especially the security operatives.
381. Don't indulge/embark on any type of jokes/hoax that will threaten security and put unnecessary pressure on the security agents, making them to be

taken off their duty posts – normal and real beats such that after investigation it turns out to be a mere hoax/fake.
382. Don't be too quick to pass judgement, for no one, not even you are perfect.
383. Don't ever take over a fight that is not yours because you think the other members of the group cannot defend themselves.
384. What is the worst that can happen to you?
385. Losing a job is not the worst that can happen to you. Therefore, encourage and comfort yourself if you have just lost your job. It has happened because a better one is on the way soon and very soon. Even if you lost your loved one/s, grieve the loss/es, but learn to move on because the reason why you now live is that you too will die someday like every mortal currently living on the planet Earth until the Day of the Lord.
386. Don't try to be a Mrs or Mr Know-all, for s/he who knows not and says that s/he knows not is a fool.
387. Had I known is a brother and sister to Mr/s Late. Therefore, always think before you act.
388. Always be prepared and ready, for you never know when that opportunity for which you have earnestly been waiting will come.
389. Always show appreciation for anything/gifts that you have received from God and people.
390. Learn to say, "Thank you!" or "I'm grateful."
391. Learn to say, "Sorry," when you are wrong, or get it wrong.

392. Whenever you are on life's highway waiting to cross to the other side of the road of life, you must do well to wait for the greenlight before crossing.
393. Don't let anyone rob you of your childhood by taking you to your local chicken and chips shop for just a can of soft drink and a box of chicken and chips. Therefore, be mindful of the consequences and your future.
394. Say "No" to 'youth violence'.
395. People who don't look like you shouldn't be labelled as 'monkeys' and be thrown banana pills at. Excepting the colour of their skins which attests to the fact that variety is the spice of life, there's just no difference between you and them. After all, all human beings migrated from Africa to their present abodes in the world. You must always bear in mind that black, white and brown are all human beings created by (one) God. We are all members of the human race and human brotherhood and family, colours and cultures notwithstanding.
396. Why be proud and why look down on others just because you are making a quick head start in life? Do you not know that if you succeed, you succeed for yourself?
397. Don't ever write anybody off or regard them as failures, not even a corpse lying by the roadside, for they can make eternity, whilst you with all your arrogance, pomposity, self-righteousness and self-delusion languish in hell. Therefore, do you not know that in the universe of God, every star has their time and place?

398. Don't talk above the other person.
399. Stop! Don't feed on rubbish?
400. Again, what is the worst that can ever happen to you?
401. Cultivate the notebook habit, drawing up your to-do list day by day, scoring and rewarding yourself at the end of each day.
402. Set goals for yourself, write down your visions and work towards achieving them.
403. Set yourself daily targets and cultivate the habit of using a 'To-do list,' – score/grade yourself on daily basis from 0–100% and celebrate yourself when you have your targets met.
404. It is not when, how, why and from where you start, but how you end.
405. Never gather in the alleyway to do drugs or engage in any form of criminal activities or just hang around with your peers/friends idly doing nothing, for you do scare pedestrians to death whenever you hang around there purposelessly.
406. Also, keep off the subway, for it is not for purposeless or aimless gathering. Remember that you are not expected to hide there and be doing drugs or carry out any nefarious activities.
407. Forward ever and backward never.
408. No human being or circumstances of life is/are strong enough to stop you, but you yourself.
409. Don't rudely interrupt a conversation between one person and another. But if it is something urgent you want to pass across to anyone of the

conversationalists, then you must politely ask for a permission to take their attention away.

410. If you want to engage a known or an unknown person in a conversation or want help from them, you must politely say, "Please can I take a moment of your time?" or "May I take a moment of your time please?" or "Could I take a moment of your time please?" or "Can I borrow a sec?"

411. Always cultivate the habit of saying "Please" whenever you want something or a favour from someone. Examples: "Please can you pass me the plate?" or "You couldn't pass me the plate please?" You can also say, "May I have you pass me the plate please?" or "May I have that plate please?" or "Could you please give me that/the plate?"

412. If you want to go ahead of someone on the pedestrian lane because you think they are blocking your way or you are in a hurry, so want someone, say a pedestrian to give way or make a way for you to enable you pass, say, "Excuse me please!" Or simply say, "Sorry," in a very polite and pleasant/friendly tone. This is better than clapping very rudely or making a very rude sound or scaring them off the way.

413. Don't resort to playing up racial card any time you lose an argument or whenever you meet a more intelligent person than you.

414. Always appreciate people, even if not of your race, and their natural giftings/endowment.

415. Don't be jealous of others, their achievements and talents. Always do well to avoid petty jealousy, for

it eats your soul like a corrosive acid and the story of Cain and Abel should be a lesson for you as you course through this life because petty jealousy/envy can lead you to kill someone!

416. Stop lying. You better don't lie because the lie you tell will germinate, bear lots of fruits, and undoubtedly you will be the first to eat its fruits.

417. You show yourself thoroughly stupid in the eyes of those you always assume they know nothing, whatsoever, simply because they are of a different race and culture.

418. Don't throw away money just to please your friends and feel good for whatever reason/s, for there will come a time in your life when you will look for just those coins you are throwing away so easily today, that you will not find them. Life is not what you are taking it in your teens. What is more, that money you are throwing away easily, there are some people on the other side of the Atlantic, looking for it but can't find it.

419. When you go shopping, any coins that you don't need, don't throw them away, but put them in the charity coins box kept in your local store.

420. Don't be a vandal, going about vandalising things – vandalising public properties, memorials, statues, etc.

421. Don't let any person look down on you because of your age.

422. Don't get involved in football hooliganism or acts of hooliganism.

423. God is not interested in the supremacy of any race, but in the oneness and equality of all persons, no matter their race, religion, creed or philosophy.
424. If you have a will like a grain of mustard seed, there is a way as gigantic as the mighty Leviathan and as high as the sky.
425. Don't follow fashion or anything in vogue.
426. Dare to be different!
427. The future is not tomorrow nor a distant time, but now.
428. Stand tall, walk tall, so you can stand up and be counted.
429. No skating on the shop floor.
430. There's no such thing as a particular generation is born at the right time. Therefore, every generation is rightly born because it was the right time for each generation to be born.
431. Aim high!
432. Dream big.
433. Never ever indulge in self-harm.
434. Work and pray hard to become the person you want to become.
435. Don't bury your talent.
436. Never ever compare yourself with anyone that is making rapid progress in life, perhaps faster than you are making.
437. I am me – the ever beautiful me and the ever wonderful me – fearfully me; the peculiar me; the royal me; the upright me; different me; unique me; incomparable me and there is no one like me on the surface of the earth. I'm, therefore, not a photocopy

or an echo of any human being on the planet earth, but a being created only in the image of my Maker.
438. Learn from your mistakes.
439. Don't allow yourself to be deceived by the 'perfect life apostles' because there is no such a thing, and there has never been such a thing as 'the perfect life'. Life is full of imperfections and it is that imperfection that defines it, hence imperfection is life and life is imperfections!
440. What is the good life, but the life of contentment with a peace of mind that surpasses all understanding? You must, therefore, be content with life and what life has offered you.
441. Who is great, but that gentle, quiet and humble soul with an unparalleled capacity to convert their I-ism to thou and we-isms.
442. If I became the leader of my country and I do not govern them well, what will happen to my fellow citizens?
443. Aim to be in harmony with yourself, your neighbours and the world around you by maintaining a harmonious vertical relationship with your Creator and an equally harmonious, but horizontal relationship with your environment and all of its biotic contents – persons (your neighbours) and other creatures/objects (other forms of life).
444. Henceforth, say to ten of your friends each day after you have greeted them, "I'll see you at the top."

445. If someone tries to, on their own free will, render you help, don't turn around and say to them, "I didn't ask for it."
446. Be diligent.
447. Be vigilant.
448. Watch what you watch.
449. Watch what you see.
450. And Watch what you listen to.
451. Stop feeding on rubbish! (What you eat and read.)
452. Show me a person who never makes mistake and I'll tell you who they are.
453. Don't eat your lemon but make lemonade out of it.
454. Make sure you don't do anything to disrupt the cycle of your youth, preventing it from running its full course.
455. Don't take your bike inside when you go shopping at your local supermarket store, or ride your scooter whilst inside or skate therein as you could get yourself or others hurt and maimed for life in the event of an accident.
456. Never say die!
457. Never give up!
458. Never quit!
459. Hold strong and keep on keeping on.
460. Never give up trying, for there is no harm in trying, not even in you keep trying.
461. Work hard and succeed at last.
462. If you have a violent boy/girlfriend/partner, let any of your loved ones or close confidants or the police know about it. On this occasion, you are not reporting them but helping them.

463. When you go shopping at your local supermarket, don't take your dog/puppy in, for only guide dogs are allowed inside. This rule is for public health reason – health and safety.
464. Whenever you are taking your dog for a walk, respect other people's right of way. Remember, you are to shorten /adjust your dog's leash/lead line when a road user like you is approaching. This must be done for persons of all races/cultures and not only members of your race, whilst you deliberately fail to adjust your dog's tether, thinking very wrongly that the person coming might attack you, just because they are not of your race.
465. Always bear in mind that your right stops where mine begins.
466. Don't ever use deprecatory words on yourself such as:
    - I'm no good or not good at anything.
    - I'm useless or I'm totally useless.
    - I'm bad or I'm very bad.
    - I'm lazy.
    - I'm worthless or I'm thoroughly worthless.
    - I'm rubbish/My life is rubbish.
    - I'm not fit for purpose.
    - I just don't know why I'm here.
    - My life is thoroughly without meaning.
    - My life isn't worth a dime.
    - I'll kill myself, life's too, too hard and not worth living.

- Better to die than to exist.
- I want to end it all and call it quit!
- I'm a mess/I'm messed up/My life is a mess!
- In fact, I'm foolish and I think I'm.

467. In your life, journey up the ladder of greatness, make sure you don't deliberately choose to miss a step because missing a step means missing all steps. And if this happens, you are sure to crash-land and start all over again. But if you are to arrogantly refuse to start all over again, then you may have to remain at the base or at the zero rung of the ladder perpetually.

468. Don't drink-drive. Make sure you keep to the official speed limit whenever you are driving, lest you run fowl of the law.

469. If you hate people, it is because you first hate yourself. Correspondingly, if you love yourself, you will love others.

470. Never ever, spike anyone's drink either at parties, in the pubs or anywhere else.

471. If you are of age, ensure you do not get addicted to scratch cards. And if it is possible, avoid it completely.

472. Don't ever gamble! Again, I say to you, "Never ever gamble!"

473. Ne'er mind nor worry, for it will be fine and you'll be alright henceforth.

474. It shall be well with you.

475. All will soon be over.

476. Don't offer yourself as a mule for drugs.

477. Be you and let me be me.

478. Don't run another person's race but run your race to the finish line.
479. If you are in a peer group and you always feel disgusted at their bad behaviours or their behavioural tendencies and do feel odd amongst them, then you are in a wrong peer group and you must get out of such a group immediately because that is not where you belong.
480. If you are not into a marriage, say so to your friend and don't purpose to keep any man as a gigolo.
481. Never ever commit suicide or attempt to take your life for any reason whatsoever. You must value your life and consider the pains you are likely to put your loved ones through carrying such act against yourself.
482. Don't embark on self-harm.
483. Don't stay in the alleyway to do drugs or hang out there for any reason whatsoever because you do scare people whenever you do.
484. Don't go to your local supermarket and buy products and after having paid and consumed it half way, you return it afterwards to customer assistants, asking for a refund lying the product is not good or ask for a refund for the same reason after having consumed it half way.
485. Don't fly-tip at the car park of your local supermarket, for you could get yourself hurt, get knocked down by vehicles coming in and going out or run into cars trying to park or get out of the car park.

486. Know who you are so that nobody tosses you about like a plankton under the flotsam and jetsam of life.
487. Stand tall and walk tall.
488. Believe; in yourself believe. Again, I say, "Believe in yourself."
489. Don't let anyone force you to do bad things.
490. You will succeed if you work hard and pray.
491. Keep off rubbish or rotten communications.
492. Never take delight or plot to avenge anyone who has wronged you because you think vengeance is sweet.
493. Pay attention to your parents' teachings and instructions and learn from their mistakes and swallow up their advice as a giant sea predator would swallow up or devour its prey. Work on their advice and let them nourish your body and become like the dew and balm upon your soul and bring you everlasting peace of mind.
494. We are all counter-terror, anti-radicalisation warriors and crime fighters generally – and securing a nation is the responsibility of everybody.
495. If a human being cannot recognise a fellow human being, then that fellow human being who fails to recognise the other human being as a human being is no more a human being but a beast.
496. You really don't need a fellow human being to validate your humanity or existence, for you had already been validated by your Maker even before you were formed in the womb as "Fearfully, wonderfully, beautifully made." – Psalms 139:14,

and "…a chosen people, a royal priesthood, a holy nation, God's special possession, that you may declare the praises of him who called you out of darkness into his wonderful light." – 1 Peter 2:9, "and had had the stamp and the signature of your Maker/Creator stamped on you as 'very good'." – Genesis 1:31

497. Don't quit because quitters never win, but the hardworking, the dedicated, the diligent, the determined and those who persevere till the end do always win.

498. Desire money for the good that you can use money to do and never money for money's sake or wealth for wealth's sake.

499. Be aware that in life, something can go right as well as go wrong.

500. My definition of life is that, that is smooth and that that is rough.

501. It is not possible for you to be right all the time just as it is not possible for you to be wrong all the time.

502. Nothing is wrong with your skin even if it is as black as a charcoal, or with you yourself as a person and as a member of a particular race and culture. So also, nothing is wrong with your nose even if it is as flat as a plateau and as big as Mount Olympus or as pointed as a spike. In a similar vein, if your skin is as pink as a type of rose flower, this is who you have been created to be with such an outer covering without having to apologise to anyone for the colour of your skin. On the other hand, if your skin is as brown as a berry and your

nose as little as a grain of mustard seed, it does not matter and you shouldn't and mustn't have to apologise to another human being like you for your look or for how you have been created to be and look like or wish you had the colour of the one condemning your skin colour or feel inferior because of your colour or the way you are and the way you look. That's who you are and that's just who you are – and its high time you got to accept the beautiful you just as you are, no matter your race, culture and physique. You are, in fact, the most beautiful you – not an echo or a photocopy of anyone, created in the very image of your infallible Creator/Marker. O what a masterpiece, then are you; a *magnum opus* and *primus inter pares* and there's no one like you on the surface of the Earth, and either beneath or above – and even when you are dead and gone, another you cannot appear/emerge on the scene or arise to take your place!

503. Also, 'nothing' is wrong with your accent either, whether heavy or light because your accent was primarily designed to communicate very effectively and flawlessly in your first language and 'not', repeat, and 'not' your second language which is just an acquired language. All race and psychological warfare warriors are sickos!

504. Don't embark on anorexic lifestyle all because you want to copy the lifestyle of your admired social influencers/celebrities as seen by you on the social media.

505. If you go shopping at your local supermarket and you happen to have been called back by the security operatives after you had 'purchased' some items because your contactless did not go through, simply apologise and appreciate the security operatives' vigilance. But don't lapse into tantrums thoroughly dressing them down and start abusing them for doing their job well by calling you back, thus helping to save the client company of their employers some amount of money that could have been lost through your hastiness in not waiting to see that your contactless had gone through and with you subsequently receiving your receipt before exiting. Having been brought back into the store to ensure payment, don't you ever go back to the security operatives just to exert undue authority over them by asking forcefully, disdainfully and disrespectfully, "Is that okay?", "Is that okay, eh?", "Is that alright?" This is tantamount to taking advantage of them for the simple reason that you think they are not of your race or just because you consider them doing a lowly paid job compared to yours, so had no right to have called you back in the first instance, and for any reason whatsoever.
506. Be content with whatever you've got or that life has offered you.
507. Apply moderation in all things and let the motto of every young person be: 'nothing in excess'.
508. Too much religion in the head is dangerous, but even a mustard seed godliness is great gain.
509. A sound youth is a sound nation;

510. A total youth is a total nation;
511. And a whole youth is a whole nation.
512. More, a sound mind is only to be found in a sound body – *Mens sana in corpore sano.*
513. Criticism is life and life is criticism. This means that whatever you do in life will receive an avalanche of criticisms from all and sundry. Therefore, why not go ahead and do that positive, legitimate and honest thing/cause within the bounds of the law and all the ethical principles governing such a plan or project of yours or good cause of yours and be criticised for it anyhow?
514. If you borrow a pen from a stranger to write something, return it to them after you have finished and say, "Thank you!" But don't run away with the pen because that is theft! If the pen was borrowed in an office setting or on the shop floor and you fail to return it after use, it means you have rendered that generous worker useless for the day, and are likely to put their job on the line, especially if that person does not have money to buy another pen immediately and worse if they can't get someone in their office/shop from whom to borrow.
515. Don't ever borrow money just to feed your extravagant lifestyle but borrow money to invest.
516. Be a world changer.
517. With your two fishes and five loaves of bread, feed the world!
518. Don't ever set a booby trap for any man and lure them into a marriage, expecting they will come and pay all the debts that you had by your greed,

selfishness and trademark extravagant lifestyle incurred over the years as this will crash the marriage as soon as it is consummated, because it will not take long for the man to discover you have deceived him into the marriage for this purpose. A word is enough for the wise.

519. Giving up is not only not an option, but a crime against God, yourself, humanity and posterity.

520. Don't run away from your goal nor abandon your God-given purpose. You must always plan and work hard to fulfil your God-given destiny.

521. Be aware that some hooded kids that do hang out in groups on roadsides, street corners, on pedestrian lanes/paths, at rivers paths, in the alleyways, subways, in parks, car parks, public gardens, etc, do so in order to provoke a fight. Therefore, being security conscious means using your judgement to continue your journey in their way or change course or keep off or avoid entirely such 'occupied territories'. But if you are convinced, no potential harm/danger could be in the offing, then keep calm and proceed on your course.

522. The bumpy road to your future lieth in front of you and not behind you. Therefore, don't and never ever look back on this thy odyssey.

523. Every supermarket in accordance with government legislations has policies for age restricted products, so if you are blessed with the gift of eternal youthful look, do not take offence immediately when a representative of your local supermarket

asks you for proof of age, but just cooperate and do what you have been asked to do.

524. Don't hang around your local supermarket store till their closing time – 23:00, waiting to beat up a security officer or a staff whom you had verbal exchanges with during their day or night shift or actually follow them to the bus stop or train station, irritatingly provoking them by flashing your very powerful torch light into their eyes. This is an act of intimidation and threat, and potentially a crime.

525. Never ever inject yourself with drugs or any other substance to keep you high.

526. Keep off football hooliganism and don't ever embark on racist chants during sporting tournaments.

527. A Message to the racist: A monkey will recognise another monkey, just as a human being will recognise another human being, accept, appreciate and celebrate them.

528. All hate speeches are bad and do potentially put a sword on human relationship. Therefore, be a peacemaker in your little corner and never be a purveyor of hate speech/es.

529. If you are driving, the law expects you to stop for everybody/creature when you get to a zebra crossing and not just for members of your race. It is simply racism when you drive pass without the slightest courtesy and consideration to stop at a zebra crossing, just because the people waiting to cross to the other side are not of the same race as you.

530. The internet is a useful platform for education and personal advancement, therefore, use it very wisely and very responsibly. Never ever visit dark sites just as you would never visit dark places in the real world.

531. You must resist the temptation of wanting to become a superhero in volatile, crisis and conflict-ridden regions of the world because of the inherent dangers and the attendant grave consequences.

532. Stop upskirting now! It is a crime. You must always learn to respect the dignity of women.

533. Don't ever take drugs or any substance hoping it will keep you awake in order to read for your tests or exams or for any other purpose. It may become the beginning of a very bad habit capable of messing up your life and destiny.

534. Danger! Danger! Danger! Don't keep hopping up and down the railway tracks or crisscross them to show-off to your girlfriend/boyfriend or peer group, confident no train is in sight at the time of your foolery, for you might sure end up fatally. Be careful! Be warned! Also, do ensure that you do not for reasons of taking a short cut, or dodging payment of fares or just to display stupid bravery to your girlfriend/boyfriend or peer group ever cross the rail tracks from one platform to another, and then do the most bizarre thing of jumping over the iron gate or the wall with spikes atop. Some young persons have done this and ended fatally.

535. You must not, repeat, you must not whilst in your local supermarket remove a product from its

original shelf and dump it on another shelf which is in another aisle for the fun of it or to make your friends laugh, for it gives wrong impression about product movement on the shop floor to both the security operatives and staff as they may record it against a dump-to-steal later item.

536. Don't ever place your leg on a chiller/freezer, shelf or on a vegetable basket to do your shoelace in your local supermarket because it is unhygienic to so do. You must always be health and safety conscious.

537. Always do ensure you pay for carrier bags used whenever you go shopping as they are 'Bags of help' whose proceeds go to the funding of local projects by your local supermarkets. No one hates supporting a worthy project. But do you? So why not support a worthy cause?

538. Don't turn public drivers into jokes and objects of ridicule, where you and your peer group will taunt, deride and ridicule or make jest of them. You must learn to appreciate the fact that they are the nation's economic and social drivers. The seats whereon they sit are their offices – you must therefore respect their offices.

539. Don't let your name enter criminal record for any reasons whatsoever. Wearing a tag which limits your movement because of a crime you have committed mustn't become a badge of honour in which you are to glory, but should be a badge of shame, dishonour and an embarrassment.

540. Again, do always ensure you pay for your carrier bags – otherwise known and referred to as, 'bags

of help' – when in your local shop to shop, for their proceeds go to the funding of community projects. Therefore, why not support such worthy projects.

541. Be aware that in life, every now and then, circumstances, conditions and events of life will change and likely push you to the limit, to the point of extremity and a point of exhaustion, but do bear in mind that whenever these times do occur in your life, suicide is not, and cannot and should not and 'must' never be an option. Therefore, look on the bright side of life and always do be optimistic and keep looking on the bright side of life, and do keep on, keeping on, for 'no condition is permanent in this world!'

LETTER TO MY YOUNG MUSLIM FRIEND ON THE ROAD TO IGNOMINIOUS MATYRDOM AND PERDITION

(A meditation on how to refuse to be radicalized)

BY JOHN ODEY ADUMA, BRITISH CHEVENING SCHOLAR AND PUBLISHER OF VIGILANCE, THE WORLD'S LEADING SECURITY MAGAZINE

Michael Adebolajo, one of the jailed killers of Lee Rigby with a blood-soaked hand and his blade of shame in the other… No Sanctuary for the Mujahideen!

Dear *Mujahideen,

I hear you are about to embark on a mission to 'martyrdom', but please pause and read this meditation before you begin your journey of no-return:

Never, never, never ever kill because every life is sacred to God.

Allah can fight for himself;

No true Muslim will preach hatred,

Islam is a religion of peace, therefore, don't clothe it with innocent blood,

Foreign campaigners exist to contend for the liberty of humanity and bring peace to our world;

Report all jihadi recruiters from near and far-flung lands to the police and dissociate yourself from them;

When greedy recruiters approach you through your imams and some unwary friends of yours to do the dirty job of killing for which they have collected money from blood-thirsty, beastly and crassly insensitive demons (persons), just tell them **D.I.Y:

Go and do it yourself,

Go on the bloody mission yourself,

Or send your loved ones if you so love Allah;

Don't feed on the rubbish posted on the internet by misguided *Mujahideens* and those vomited by hate preachers,

Love your neighbour as yourself;

If you cannot bomb/stab/cut/kill yourself with the bomb/blade and gun of shame,

Then don't do it to your neighbour.

In life, don't aim at bringing sorrow upon your family and humanity,

For you are their joy and the joy of the whole world!

Promote peace from and in your little corner,

And never use violence to redeem violence,

As a good citizen of your country,

Report to the police and trusted imams all threats of violence and potential threats to national security wherever they exist that you are aware of.

Be your brother's and sister's keeper,

Blood for many virgins, and blood for *Aljanah* is absolute rubbish;

Seek martyrdom only for worthy causes and feats,

And ONLY if it will glorify Allah.

Never ever involve and indulge in things that will bring your family community and international shame and ridicule;

Don't take part in terrorism and in any terror activities,

Renounce your membership of all terror cells in your local area and elsewhere;

Be angry about things you feel very passionate about, especially if they don't come as expected,

But don't be bitter as your bitterness can lead you to hate people and hatred can lead you to do unpredictable and shameful things;

HENCEFORTH, turn all your negativities to positivities,

Love life and don't love death,

Allah will love you to be alive to do his good deeds

To all humanity than see you die in a shameful cause.

Therefore, promote life and not death,

Preach love and not hatred,

Tell your friends and others about your faith lovingly and in a friendly manner;

But don't force them to embrace it or be bitter and develop hatred for them,

Especially when they refuse to accept Islam as there could be another opportunity to present Islam to them another day!

Publish your message in literature and keep its contents within the laws of your/host country and Koran and distribute them lovingly and with a smile on your face to people you come across;

Whenever you want to introduce your friends, neighbours and colleagues to Islam,

Do so by inviting them to have breakfast, lunch or dinner with you.

And afterward present Islam kindly and lovingly to them,

But certainly NOT through violence as that will grieve Allah.

If you ignore this advice and do violence and kill people,

Everyone around you will abandon you and you will be left ALONE!

Endeavour to have a confidant or a mentor in anyone you respect,

And any time you are embittered by anything,

Confide in them your anger and worries;

Always occupy your mind with serious things;

Don't join bad company;

Don't bury your talents, but do give expressions to them positively,

Be zealous for your faith, but temper it with consideration for others' faiths,

And let this be based on knowledge, sound doctrine, love and friendship.

Bring creativity to bear on all that you think, do and say;

Always be in the company of good and aspiring friends and positive people.

Remember always that you belong to the broad family of mankind – race, colour, culture, religion creed notwithstanding,

No matter what, keep hope alive at all times,

And always be positive as there's light at the end of every tunnel,

Work hard and pray,

Labour and wait,

Shun idleness because Satan always finds work for an idle hand,

Be patient, for your time will surely come one day!

Always invest your time wisely,

AND never hang around in streets, at supermarkets and on estates doing nothing,

Seek wisdom, knowledge and understanding – make your local library your 'home' or a place you will always visit to satisfy this quest and thirst.

STOP! Don't rush life and if you do, life will rush you!

NEVER live on the fast lane of life as doing so will lead to your dying young.

Do a little at a time,

Aim high by dreaming big, but let your dream be realistic,

Commit into writing, things you feel very passionately about – publish them in pamphlets, booklets, books and distribute them – or start a blog or twit such,

Start literary and debating club in your locality/neighbourhood where you can debate your ideas with like minds – or go to TV houses and discuss them or write to newspapers editors,

ALWAYS read books that will challenge you positively,

Adopt a hero/role model, dead or alive – Abraham Lincoln, Mandela, Churchill, Gandhi, Mother Theresa, etc.

Don't do anything in excess;

Don't let any person exploit or take advantage of your youth,

But be an example of a good citizen and a good Muslim,

Prepare for tomorrow from where you are right now because the future is NOW!

Do not live big without commensurate income,

And don't emulate what is wrong,

Never try to be a hero,

Sleep in time – say 9 p.m. and aim at having a good night's sleep,

Don't do drug, nor religion nor ***humanligion*, but do God ALWAYS!

Respect yourself, respect others and be yourself always – but never try to run another person's race or be an echo of somebody,

Obey your parents and obey constituted authorities too,

DON'T rebel for the sake of it, but be a rebel with a cause,

Be the change you want to see in your little corner,

Work and pray – play and work for this is good for your overall health and spiritual well-being,

Don't aim at a better world, but aim ALWAYS to make the world a better place in which to live,

Treat others as if they were you and even better than yourself.

Have a goal, have a purpose and don't be a floater on the ocean of life -

ALWAYS ask yourself these questions: WHO AM I? WHY AM I HERE ON EARTH? WHAT IS THE PURPOSE OF LIFE? WHAT WILL I DO IN MY LITTLE CORNER TO MAKE A DIFFERENCE IN THE WORLD?

Build and don't destroy – and add when necessary – BUT subtract ONLY when necessary,

If anyone offends you, don't burst into flames immediately,

But count up to 5000 times and then leave the vexed scene and the people that have annoyed you.

Do a little at a time and take a step at a time,

And always remember – a journey of a thousand miles begin with a step.

And do REMEMBER too that a sound mind can only to be found in a sound body!

*Mujahideen – strugglers or jihadists/those who fight on behalf of the Muslim faith – Islam or fellow Muslims (the (ummah).

**D.I.Y – do it yourself.

***Humanligion – man-based faith; misinterpretation of God-based religions according to sense knowledge and human emotions leading to conflicts and killings; zeal for one's religion without knowledge and understanding.

The Good Youth's Good Character Pledge

My Resolution:
    Henceforth, I'm resolved to turn over a new leaf
    And not just become good for myself or for the sake of it,
    But for the sake of my family, the nation and the world.
    Henceforth, my name is ambition,
    And from now on, I'm resolved to be ambitious,
    I will work hard, pray hard and aspire to be great and to do great things for myself, family, the nation and all of humanity.
    Henceforth, I'm resolved to add to life and not to subtract it:
    Either by words or deeds – swords, guns or through chemical substances!
    And upon the realisation that I'm greater and grander than the gun, Samurai sword or any form of such other blade of violence and shame,
    I'm resolved to do all within me to save, nurture and preserve life – human life and all of life forms.
    Therefore, I'm resolved to be a good youth and a good person, and a good citizen of my country and of the world;
    And an ambassador for peace and justice.

Above all, I will henceforth be an evangelist for universal altruism.

So, help me God.

Date..

Name...,............

Signed..

Epilogue

"Those who spare the rod of discipline, hate their children. Those who love their children, care enough to discipline them."

— *Proverbs 13:24*

The End